62 African Recipes for Home

By: Kelly Johnson

Table of Contents

- Jollof Rice (West Africa)
- Fufu and Light Soup (West Africa)
- Bobotie (South Africa)
- Bunny Chow (South Africa)
- Doro Wat (Ethiopia)
- Kitfo (Ethiopia)
- Chapati (East Africa)
- Nyama Choma (East Africa)
- Piri Piri Chicken (Mozambique)
- Cachupa (Cape Verde)
- Maafe (West Africa)
- Biltong (South Africa)
- Moroccan Tagine (Morocco)
- Shawarma (North Africa)
- Bobo de Camarao (Mozambique)
- Acheke (Ivory Coast)
- Kelewele (Ghana)
- Brik (Tunisia)
- Muamba de Galinha (Angola)
- Mafé (Senegal)
- Samosa (North Africa)
- Pap en Vleis/Shisa Nyama (South Africa)
- Chermoula (North Africa)
- Domoda (Gambia)
- Bambara Beans Soup (Nigeria)
- Berbere Chicken (Eritrea)
- Atayef (North Africa)
- Efo Riro (Nigeria)
- Kushari (Egypt)
- Dibi (Senegal)
- Lentil Wat (Ethiopia)
- Mango Curry Chicken (Mauritius)
- Nsala Soup (Congo)
- Suya (Nigeria)
- Kefta Tagine (Morocco)
- Papaya Salad (East Africa)

- Akara (West Africa)
- Chicken Yassa (Senegal)
- Koshari (Sudan)
- Mozambican Prawn Curry (Mozambique)
- Plasas (Liberia)
- Braaivleis (South Africa)
- Sosatie (South Africa)
- Kedjenou (Ivory Coast)
- Dolma (North Africa)
- Kitcha Fit-Fit (Eritrea)
- Yassa Poulet (Senegal)
- Tajine el Khodar (Algeria)
- Efo Elegusi (Nigeria)
- Fried Tilapia (Ghana)
- Kahawa (East Africa)
- Sorpotel (Goa, influenced by African cuisine)
- Ogbono Soup (Nigeria)
- Chakalaka (South Africa)
- Moin Moin (Nigeria)
- Kunu (Nigeria)
- Okro Soup (West Africa)
- Pulao (North Africa)
- Bissap Juice (Senegal)
- Chibwantu (Zambia)
- Amagwinya/Vetkoek (South Africa)
- Nsima (Malawi)

Jollof Rice (West Africa)

Ingredients:

- 2 cups long-grain parboiled rice
- 1/4 cup vegetable oil
- 1 large onion, finely chopped
- 3-4 large tomatoes, blended or grated
- 1 red bell pepper, blended or grated
- 1 green bell pepper, blended or grated
- 2-3 cloves of garlic, minced
- 1 teaspoon ginger, grated
- 1 teaspoon thyme
- 1 teaspoon curry powder
- 2 bay leaves
- 2 cups chicken or vegetable broth
- Salt and pepper to taste

Instructions:

Prepare the Rice:
- Rinse the rice in cold water until the water runs clear to remove excess starch.

Prepare the Tomato Base:
- Blend or grate the tomatoes, red bell pepper, and green bell pepper to create a smooth mixture.

Cooking the Base:
- In a large pot, heat the vegetable oil over medium heat.
- Add the chopped onions and sauté until they become translucent.

Add Aromatics:
- Add the minced garlic and grated ginger to the onions. Sauté for another minute until fragrant.

Tomato Mixture:
- Pour in the blended or grated tomato and pepper mixture. Cook for about 10-15 minutes, stirring occasionally, until the mixture thickens, and the oil begins to separate.

Spices:
- Add thyme, curry powder, bay leaves, salt, and pepper to the tomato mixture. Stir well to combine.

Parboiled Rice:

- Add the rinsed parboiled rice to the pot and stir, ensuring the rice is well-coated with the tomato mixture.

Broth:
- Pour in the chicken or vegetable broth. Stir well and bring the mixture to a gentle boil.

Simmer:
- Reduce the heat to low, cover the pot with a tight-fitting lid, and simmer for about 20-25 minutes or until the rice is cooked and has absorbed the liquid.

Check for Doneness:
- Occasionally check the rice to prevent sticking to the bottom of the pot. You can add more broth or water if needed.

Fluff and Serve:
- Once the rice is cooked, fluff it with a fork to separate the grains. Remove the bay leaves.

Serve:
- Serve the Jollof Rice hot, garnished with additional chopped fresh vegetables if desired.

Jollof Rice is often served with grilled or fried chicken, fish, or other protein sources. Enjoy this flavorful and vibrant West African dish!

Fufu and Light Soup (West Africa)

Fufu Ingredients:

- 2 cups cassava flour or yam flour
- Water for cooking

Light Soup Ingredients:

- 1 lb assorted meats (chicken, goat meat, or beef), cut into bite-sized pieces
- 1 large onion, chopped
- 3 tomatoes, chopped
- 1 red or green bell pepper, chopped
- 2 cloves garlic, minced
- 1-inch ginger, grated
- 2 tablespoons vegetable oil
- 1 teaspoon ground cayenne pepper (adjust to taste)
- 1 teaspoon ground coriander
- 1 teaspoon ground cumin
- 1 teaspoon dried thyme
- 2 bay leaves
- Salt and pepper to taste
- 6 cups water or chicken broth
- Fresh herbs (such as parsley or cilantro) for garnish

Instructions:

Fufu Preparation:

    Boil Water:
- Bring a pot of water to a boil.

    Mix Fufu Flour:
- In a separate bowl, mix the cassava or yam flour with a small amount of cold water to form a smooth, thick paste.

    Cook Fufu:
- Slowly add the fufu paste to the boiling water, stirring continuously to avoid lumps.
- Cook and stir until the fufu thickens and reaches a smooth consistency.

    Shape Fufu:

- Allow the fufu to cool slightly, then wet your hands and shape the fufu into smooth, round balls or oval shapes.

Light Soup Preparation:

Brown Meat:
- In a large pot, heat the vegetable oil over medium heat. Brown the assorted meats until they are well-seared on all sides.

Add Aromatics:
- Add chopped onions, minced garlic, and grated ginger to the pot. Sauté until the onions are translucent.

Tomato and Pepper Mixture:
- Stir in chopped tomatoes, chopped bell pepper, ground cayenne pepper, ground coriander, ground cumin, dried thyme, bay leaves, salt, and pepper.

Simmer:
- Pour in water or chicken broth and bring the mixture to a simmer. Allow it to cook for about 20-30 minutes, allowing the flavors to meld.

Adjust Seasoning:
- Taste the soup and adjust the seasoning if necessary.

Add Vegetables (Optional):
- You can add vegetables like spinach, okra, or other greens to the soup and cook until they are tender.

Finish and Serve:
- Garnish the soup with fresh herbs and serve hot with the fufu on the side.

To eat, tear off a small piece of the fufu, form it into a small ball, and use it to scoop up the light soup. Fufu and Light Soup is a hearty and comforting dish enjoyed in many West African countries.

Bobotie (South Africa)

Ingredients:

For the Meat Mixture:

- 1 kg ground beef or lamb
- 2 slices of white bread
- 1 cup milk
- 2 tablespoons vegetable oil
- 2 onions, finely chopped
- 2 cloves garlic, minced
- 1 tablespoon curry powder
- 1 tablespoon ground turmeric
- 1 tablespoon ground coriander
- 1 teaspoon ground cumin
- 1 teaspoon ground cinnamon
- 1/2 cup raisins
- 1/4 cup apricot jam
- 2 tablespoons white vinegar
- Salt and pepper to taste

For the Topping:

- 2 large eggs
- 1 cup milk
- 1/4 teaspoon ground turmeric (for color)

For Serving:

- Cooked yellow rice
- Chutney (optional)

Instructions:

Preheat Oven:
- Preheat your oven to 180°C (350°F).

Prepare Bread and Milk Mixture:
- In a bowl, soak the bread slices in 1 cup of milk until it's well-soaked.

Prepare Meat Mixture:

- Heat vegetable oil in a pan over medium heat. Add chopped onions and garlic, sauté until softened.

Add Spices:
- Add curry powder, ground turmeric, ground coriander, ground cumin, and ground cinnamon to the onion mixture. Cook for 2-3 minutes until fragrant.

Combine with Meat:
- In a large mixing bowl, combine the ground meat with the onion and spice mixture.

Bread Mixture:
- Squeeze excess milk from the soaked bread and add the bread to the meat mixture. Mix well.

Flavor Additions:
- Add raisins, apricot jam, white vinegar, salt, and pepper to the meat mixture. Mix thoroughly.

Transfer to Dish:
- Transfer the meat mixture to a greased baking dish and press it down evenly.

Prepare Topping:
- In a separate bowl, whisk together eggs, milk, and ground turmeric for the topping.

Pour Topping:
- Pour the egg and milk mixture over the meat mixture, ensuring it covers the entire surface.

Bake:
- Bake in the preheated oven for approximately 45-50 minutes or until the topping is set and golden brown.

Serve:
- Serve the Bobotie hot, sliced into squares or portions, with cooked yellow rice.

Optional:
- Serve with chutney on the side for an extra burst of flavor.

Bobotie is a delightful dish that captures the essence of South African cuisine. Enjoy its unique combination of spices and textures!

Bunny Chow (South Africa)

Ingredients:

For the Curry:

- 1 kg chicken, lamb, or beef, cut into bite-sized pieces (vegetarian options can include chickpeas or lentils)
- 2 tablespoons vegetable oil
- 2 large onions, finely chopped
- 3 tomatoes, chopped
- 3 tablespoons curry powder
- 1 tablespoon ground cumin
- 1 tablespoon ground coriander
- 1 teaspoon turmeric
- 4 cloves garlic, minced
- 1-inch ginger, grated
- 2-3 green chilies, chopped (adjust to taste)
- 1 cinnamon stick
- 4-5 curry leaves (optional)
- 1 can (400 ml) coconut milk
- Salt and pepper to taste
- Fresh coriander leaves for garnish

For the Bunny Chow:

- Round or oblong loaves of unsliced white bread (1 loaf per person)

Instructions:

For the Curry:

Prepare Ingredients:
- Gather and prepare all the ingredients before starting.

Brown the Meat:
- In a large pot, heat the vegetable oil over medium heat. Brown the meat pieces on all sides. Remove the meat from the pot and set it aside.

Sauté Onions:
- In the same pot, add chopped onions and sauté until they become translucent.

Add Spices:

- Add curry powder, ground cumin, ground coriander, turmeric, minced garlic, grated ginger, chopped green chilies, cinnamon stick, and curry leaves (if using). Stir well to combine.

Cook Tomatoes:
- Add chopped tomatoes and cook until they start to break down.

Return Meat to Pot:
- Return the browned meat to the pot and coat it with the spice mixture.

Add Coconut Milk:
- Pour in the coconut milk, season with salt and pepper, and stir. Bring the mixture to a simmer.

Simmer:
- Cover the pot and let the curry simmer for about 30-40 minutes or until the meat is tender and the flavors meld together.

Garnish:
- Garnish with fresh coriander leaves before serving.

For the Bunny Chow:

Prepare Bread Loaves:
- Cut a small portion from the top of each loaf to create a lid. Hollow out the center of the loaf, leaving a thick layer of bread on the sides and bottom.

Fill with Curry:
- Spoon the prepared curry into the hollowed-out bread loaves.

Serve:
- Place the lids back on top of the filled loaves and serve hot.

Bunny Chow is often eaten with the hands, tearing pieces of the bread to scoop up the delicious curry. It's a unique and flavorful dish that represents the diverse culinary influences in South Africa.

Doro Wat (Ethiopia)

Ingredients:

For the Berbere Spice Mix:

- 1 tablespoon ground paprika
- 1 tablespoon ground cayenne pepper
- 1 tablespoon ground fenugreek
- 1 tablespoon ground coriander
- 1 tablespoon ground cumin
- 1 tablespoon ground cardamom
- 1 tablespoon ground cloves
- 1 tablespoon ground allspice
- 1 tablespoon ground cinnamon
- 1 tablespoon ground nutmeg
- 1 tablespoon ground ginger
- 1 tablespoon garlic powder
- 1 tablespoon onion powder

For the Doro Wat:

- 1.5 kg chicken, cut into pieces
- 2 large red onions, finely chopped
- 4 cloves garlic, minced
- 1-inch ginger, grated
- 1 cup vegetable oil
- 1/4 cup berbere spice mix (adjust to taste)
- 1/2 cup tomato paste
- 1 cup chicken broth
- Salt to taste
- Hard-boiled eggs (optional, for garnish)
- Fresh cilantro or parsley for garnish

For Serving:

- Injera (Ethiopian sourdough flatbread)

Instructions:

For the Berbere Spice Mix:

Combine Spices:
- In a bowl, thoroughly mix together all the spices to create the berbere spice blend. Set aside.

For the Doro Wat:

Marinate Chicken:
- In a large bowl, rub the chicken pieces with 2 tablespoons of the berbere spice mix. Let it marinate for at least 30 minutes.

Sauté Onions:
- In a large pot or Dutch oven, heat the vegetable oil over medium heat. Add the finely chopped onions and cook until they become soft and golden.

Add Garlic and Ginger:
- Add minced garlic and grated ginger to the onions. Sauté for an additional 2-3 minutes until fragrant.

Add Berbere Spice:
- Stir in the remaining berbere spice mix and cook for a few minutes to release the flavors. Be cautious not to burn the spices.

Tomato Paste:
- Add the tomato paste and cook, stirring continuously, until it darkens in color and the oil starts to separate from the mixture.

Cook Chicken:
- Add the marinated chicken pieces to the pot and coat them with the spice mixture.

Simmer:
- Pour in the chicken broth, season with salt, and bring the mixture to a simmer. Cover and cook over low heat for about 45-60 minutes or until the chicken is tender and cooked through.

Garnish:
- Optionally, garnish the Doro Wat with hard-boiled eggs and fresh cilantro or parsley.

Serve:
- Serve Doro Wat hot with injera on the side.

Doro Wat is often eaten by tearing pieces of injera and using them to scoop up the delicious spicy chicken stew. It's a flavorful and iconic dish in Ethiopian cuisine.

Kitfo (Ethiopia)

Ingredients:

- 500 grams beef sirloin or tenderloin, finely minced
- 2-3 tablespoons unsalted butter, clarified
- 1-2 teaspoons mitmita (Ethiopian spice blend, can be adjusted to taste)
- 1 teaspoon ground cardamom
- Salt to taste
- 1 teaspoon ground cumin (optional)
- 1 teaspoon ground coriander (optional)
- Injera or bread for serving

Instructions:

Prepare Mitmita:
- If you don't have mitmita readily available, you can make it by combining ground red pepper, cardamom, and salt. Adjust the quantities to achieve the desired level of spiciness.

Clarify Butter:
- In a small saucepan, melt the butter over low heat. Skim off the foam and solids, leaving only the clear, clarified butter. Set aside.

Season the Meat:
- In a bowl, combine the finely minced beef with mitmita, ground cardamom, salt, and optionally, ground cumin and coriander. Mix well to ensure the spices are evenly distributed.

Warm the Butter:
- Gently warm the clarified butter, being careful not to let it brown.

Mix with Butter:
- Pour the warmed clarified butter over the seasoned meat. Mix thoroughly to combine the meat and butter, ensuring an even distribution of flavors.

Serve:
- Kitfo can be served in various ways. Traditionally, it can be shaped into a mound or a log on a plate. You can also form a well in the center and pour a little extra clarified butter into it for added richness.

Accompaniments:
- Kitfo is often served with injera or bread on the side. It's common to have additional side dishes like cottage cheese (ayib) and cooked greens (gomen) to balance the flavors.

Eat Immediately:

- Kitfo is best enjoyed immediately after preparation, while the meat is fresh and the flavors are vibrant.

Note: Some variations of Kitfo involve lightly cooking the minced meat to take the raw edge off. If you prefer a cooked version, you can quickly sauté the meat in a pan for a minute or two before mixing it with the spices.

Kitfo is a unique and flavorful dish, and its preparation can vary based on regional and personal preferences in Ethiopia. Adjust the spice levels according to your taste and enjoy this traditional Ethiopian delicacy!

Chapati (East Africa)

Ingredients:

- 2 cups all-purpose flour
- 1 cup warm water
- 2 tablespoons vegetable oil
- 1/2 teaspoon salt
- Extra flour for dusting
- Extra oil or ghee for cooking

Instructions:

Prepare the Dough:
- In a mixing bowl, combine the all-purpose flour and salt. Gradually add warm water while stirring to form a dough.
- Knead the dough on a floured surface for about 5-7 minutes until it becomes smooth and elastic.

Add Oil:
- Add 2 tablespoons of vegetable oil to the dough and continue kneading for another 3-5 minutes. The dough should be soft and slightly sticky.

Rest the Dough:
- Cover the dough with a clean kitchen towel and let it rest for at least 30 minutes. This allows the gluten to relax, making the chapatis softer.

Divide the Dough:
- Divide the rested dough into golf ball-sized portions.

Rolling Out the Chapatis:
- Take one portion of the dough and roll it into a thin, round disc on a floured surface. Aim for a thickness similar to a tortilla.

Apply Oil:
- Brush the rolled-out chapati with a thin layer of oil or ghee.

Fold and Roll:
- Fold the oiled chapati in half, then fold it again to form a quarter-circle. Roll out the folded dough into a thin, flat disc.

Cooking:
- Heat a flat griddle or a non-stick pan over medium-high heat. Place the rolled-out chapati on the hot griddle.

Cook Both Sides:
- Cook for about 1-2 minutes on each side until small brown spots appear, and the chapati puffs up. Press down with a spatula if necessary.

Apply Oil (Optional):
- If desired, brush the cooked chapati with a bit more oil or ghee.

Repeat:
- Repeat the process with the remaining portions of dough.

Keep Warm:
- Stack the cooked chapatis and keep them warm by wrapping them in a clean kitchen towel.

Serve:
- Serve the chapatis warm as a side dish or with your favorite curry.

Chapati is a wonderful accompaniment to stews, curries, or as a wrap for various fillings. Enjoy these soft and delicious East African flatbreads!

Nyama Choma (East Africa)

Ingredients:

- 1 kg beef or goat meat, cut into skewer-friendly cubes
- 1/4 cup vegetable oil
- 3 cloves garlic, minced
- 1 tablespoon ginger, grated
- 1 tablespoon paprika
- 1 teaspoon ground cayenne pepper (adjust to taste)
- 1 teaspoon ground cumin
- 1 teaspoon ground coriander
- Salt and pepper to taste
- Lemon wedges for serving

Instructions:

Prepare the Marinade:
- In a bowl, combine vegetable oil, minced garlic, grated ginger, paprika, cayenne pepper, cumin, coriander, salt, and pepper. Mix well to form a paste.

Marinate the Meat:
- Place the meat cubes in a large bowl and coat them with the marinade. Ensure that each piece is well coated. Cover the bowl with plastic wrap and let it marinate in the refrigerator for at least 2 hours, or overnight for better flavor.

Skewering the Meat:
- Preheat your grill or barbecue. If using wooden skewers, soak them in water for about 30 minutes to prevent burning.
- Thread the marinated meat cubes onto the skewers.

Grilling:
- Grill the meat skewers over medium-high heat, turning occasionally, until the meat is cooked to your desired level of doneness. This usually takes about 10-15 minutes.

Basting (Optional):
- If desired, you can baste the meat with any remaining marinade or a mixture of oil and lemon juice during the grilling process.

Resting:
- Allow the grilled meat to rest for a few minutes before serving.

Serve:

- Serve Nyama Choma hot, accompanied by lemon wedges. It's often enjoyed with side dishes like grilled vegetables, salads, or a simple dipping sauce.

Enjoy Socially:
- Nyama Choma is often a social event where friends and family gather to enjoy grilled meat together. Serve with your favorite beverages and enjoy the communal experience.

Nyama Choma is a delicious and straightforward dish, highlighting the love for grilled meats in East African cuisine. It's a perfect dish for outdoor gatherings and celebrations.

Piri Piri Chicken (Mozambique)

Ingredients:

For the Piri Piri Sauce:

- 10-12 African Bird's Eye Chilies (adjust to taste)
- 3 cloves garlic, minced
- 1 teaspoon smoked paprika
- 1 teaspoon ground cumin
- 1 teaspoon dried oregano
- 1 teaspoon sugar
- 1/4 cup red wine vinegar
- 1/2 cup olive oil
- Salt and pepper to taste

For the Chicken:

- 1 whole chicken, cut into pieces or chicken drumsticks and thighs
- Salt and pepper to season
- Olive oil for brushing

Instructions:

For the Piri Piri Sauce:

Prepare Chilies:
- Stem and deseed the African Bird's Eye Chilies if you want to reduce the heat. Wear gloves while handling the chilies to avoid irritation.

Blend Ingredients:
- In a blender or food processor, combine the chilies, minced garlic, smoked paprika, ground cumin, dried oregano, sugar, red wine vinegar, olive oil, salt, and pepper. Blend until you achieve a smooth sauce consistency.

Adjust Seasoning:
- Taste the Piri Piri sauce and adjust the salt, pepper, or other seasonings according to your preference. Set aside.

For the Chicken:

Marinate the Chicken:

- Season the chicken pieces with salt and pepper. Place them in a bowl and generously coat with some of the prepared Piri Piri sauce. Reserve some sauce for basting and serving.

Marinate Time:
- Cover the marinated chicken and let it marinate in the refrigerator for at least 2 hours or preferably overnight for better flavor absorption.

Preheat Grill:
- Preheat your grill to medium-high heat.

Grill Chicken:
- Brush the grill grates with oil to prevent sticking. Place the marinated chicken on the hot grill and cook, turning occasionally, until the chicken is fully cooked with a nice char. The internal temperature should reach 165°F (74°C).

Basting:
- During the grilling process, baste the chicken with the reserved Piri Piri sauce to enhance the flavor and keep the meat moist.

Rest and Serve:
- Allow the grilled Piri Piri chicken to rest for a few minutes before serving.

Serve:
- Serve the Piri Piri Chicken hot with additional Piri Piri sauce on the side for dipping. It pairs well with rice, vegetables, or a simple salad.

Piri Piri Chicken is known for its bold and spicy flavors, making it a popular and satisfying dish. Adjust the level of heat in the sauce according to your preference, and enjoy the taste of Mozambique!

Cachupa (Cape Verde)

Ingredients:

- 2 cups dried hominy or corn kernels
- 1/2 cup dried kidney beans (or canned beans, drained)
- 1/4 cup vegetable oil
- 1 large onion, finely chopped
- 3 cloves garlic, minced
- 2 bay leaves
- 2 chorizo sausages, sliced
- 1/2 lb pork, cubed
- 1/2 lb beef, cubed
- 1/2 lb fish (such as tuna or cod), cut into chunks
- 1 sweet potato, peeled and diced
- 1 cassava, peeled and diced
- 2 carrots, peeled and diced
- 1 plantain, peeled and sliced
- 1/2 cabbage, chopped
- Salt and pepper to taste
- Fresh parsley or cilantro for garnish

Instructions:

Prepare Hominy and Beans:
- Soak the dried hominy and kidney beans separately overnight in water. Drain and rinse before using. If using canned beans, skip this step.

Cook Beans and Hominy:
- In a large pot, combine the soaked hominy and kidney beans. Cover with water and bring to a boil. Reduce heat and simmer until both are tender, adding more water if necessary.

Sauté Onions and Garlic:
- In a separate large pot, heat vegetable oil over medium heat. Add chopped onions and minced garlic. Sauté until the onions are soft and translucent.

Add Meats:
- Add the sliced chorizo, cubed pork, and cubed beef to the pot. Cook until the meats are browned.

Incorporate Fish:
- Add the fish chunks to the pot and cook briefly until they start to firm up.

Combine Vegetables:

- Stir in the diced sweet potato, cassava, carrots, plantain, and chopped cabbage.

Mix with Cooked Hominy and Beans:
- Add the cooked hominy and kidney beans to the pot with the meats and vegetables. Mix well to combine.

Simmer:
- Season the cachupa with salt and pepper, add bay leaves, and let the mixture simmer over low heat for about 30-45 minutes. Stir occasionally and add water if needed to prevent sticking.

Check for Doneness:
- Check the doneness of the vegetables and meats. Adjust the seasoning if necessary.

Garnish and Serve:
- Garnish with fresh parsley or cilantro before serving. Cachupa is traditionally served hot.

Cachupa is often enjoyed as a communal dish during social gatherings and celebrations in Cape Verde. It reflects the cultural richness of the islands and the use of locally available ingredients.

Maafe (West Africa)

Ingredients:

- 1.5 lbs (700g) meat (chicken, lamb, or beef), cut into chunks
- 1 cup peanut butter (unsweetened and natural)
- 1 large onion, finely chopped
- 2-3 tomatoes, chopped
- 1/4 cup tomato paste
- 3 tablespoons vegetable oil
- 3-4 cups chicken or vegetable broth
- 2 sweet potatoes, peeled and diced
- 2 carrots, peeled and sliced
- 1 eggplant, diced
- 1 bell pepper, diced
- 2-3 cloves garlic, minced
- 1 tablespoon grated ginger
- 1 teaspoon ground cayenne pepper (adjust to taste)

- 1 teaspoon ground coriander
- 1 teaspoon ground cumin
- Salt and pepper to taste
- Fresh cilantro or parsley for garnish
- Cooked rice or couscous for serving

Instructions:

Prepare Peanut Base:
- In a bowl, mix the peanut butter with a cup of broth until you have a smooth, lump-free paste. Set aside.

Brown the Meat:
- In a large pot or Dutch oven, heat vegetable oil over medium-high heat. Brown the meat chunks on all sides. Remove the meat from the pot and set aside.

Sauté Onions, Garlic, and Ginger:
- In the same pot, add chopped onions and sauté until they become soft. Add minced garlic and grated ginger, and cook for another minute.

Add Tomatoes and Tomato Paste:
- Stir in the chopped tomatoes and tomato paste. Cook for about 5 minutes until the tomatoes break down and the mixture thickens.

Spices:
- Add ground cayenne pepper, ground coriander, and ground cumin. Mix well to incorporate the spices.

Reintroduce Browned Meat:
- Return the browned meat to the pot and coat it with the tomato and spice mixture.

Add Peanut Butter Mixture:
- Pour in the peanut butter and broth mixture, stirring well to combine. Bring the mixture to a simmer.

Add Vegetables:
- Add diced sweet potatoes, sliced carrots, diced eggplant, and diced bell pepper to the pot. Stir to combine.

Simmer:
- Reduce the heat to low, cover the pot, and let the stew simmer for about 30-40 minutes or until the meat and vegetables are cooked through.

Adjust Seasoning:
- Taste the Maafe and adjust the seasoning with salt and pepper as needed.

Garnish and Serve:

- Garnish the Maafe with fresh cilantro or parsley. Serve the stew hot over cooked rice or couscous.

Maafe is a rich and satisfying dish with a unique combination of flavors. It's often enjoyed as a comforting and communal meal in West African households.

Biltong (South Africa)

Ingredients:

- 2 pounds (about 1 kg) beef, thinly sliced (preferably lean cuts like sirloin or silverside)
- 1 cup malt vinegar or red wine vinegar
- 2 tablespoons Worcestershire sauce
- 2 tablespoons ground coriander
- 1 tablespoon ground black pepper
- 1 tablespoon salt (coarse salt works well)
- 1 teaspoon brown sugar
- 1 teaspoon bicarbonate of soda (baking soda)

Instructions:

Prepare the Meat:
- Slice the beef into thin strips, about 1/4 to 1/2 inch thick. Trim excess fat.

Marinate the Meat:
- In a bowl, combine malt vinegar, Worcestershire sauce, ground coriander, ground black pepper, salt, brown sugar, and bicarbonate of soda. Mix until the salt and sugar dissolve.

Coat the Meat:
- Place the beef strips in a shallow dish and coat them thoroughly with the marinade. Ensure each strip is well-covered.

Marinate Time:
- Cover the dish and let the meat marinate in the refrigerator for at least 4 hours, or preferably overnight. The longer it marinates, the more flavor it will absorb.

Preheat Oven:
- Preheat your oven to its lowest setting (usually around 140°F or 60°C).

Prepare Drying Rack:
- Place a layer of foil on the bottom of the oven to catch any drips. Set a drying rack on the top oven rack.

Hang the Meat:
- Thread the marinated beef strips onto hooks or skewers, ensuring they don't touch each other. Hang the hooks or skewers on the drying rack.

Dry in the Oven:

- Dry the biltong in the oven at the lowest setting for 4-6 hours, or until it reaches your desired level of dryness. The meat should be firm but still slightly tender.

Air-Dry (Optional):
- For additional drying, you can remove the biltong from the oven and allow it to air-dry in a cool, dry place for a day or two.

Store:
- Once fully dried, store the biltong in an airtight container or vacuum-sealed bag. It can be kept at room temperature for several weeks or refrigerated for longer shelf life.

Enjoy:
- Slice the biltong into thin strips and enjoy it as a flavorful and protein-packed snack.

Biltong is a versatile snack that can be enjoyed on its own or used to add flavor to dishes. It has become a staple in South African cuisine and is often enjoyed during social gatherings and events.

Moroccan Tagine (Morocco)

Ingredients:

- 1.5 kg chicken, cut into pieces
- 2 onions, finely chopped
- 3 cloves garlic, minced
- 1 tablespoon ginger, grated
- 2 teaspoons ground cumin
- 2 teaspoons ground coriander
- 1 teaspoon ground cinnamon
- 1 teaspoon paprika
- 1/2 teaspoon ground turmeric
- Pinch of saffron threads (optional)
- Salt and pepper to taste
- 2 tablespoons olive oil
- 1 cup chicken broth
- 1 cup tomatoes, diced
- 1/2 cup dried apricots, halved
- 1/2 cup almonds, toasted
- Fresh cilantro or parsley for garnish

Instructions:

Marinate the Chicken:
- In a bowl, combine the chicken pieces with chopped onions, minced garlic, grated ginger, ground cumin, ground coriander, ground cinnamon, paprika, ground turmeric, saffron (if using), salt, and pepper. Mix well to ensure the chicken is evenly coated. Let it marinate for at least 1 hour, or overnight in the refrigerator for more flavor.

Brown the Chicken:
- Heat olive oil in the tagine or a large, heavy-bottomed pot over medium-high heat. Brown the marinated chicken pieces on all sides.

Add Broth and Tomatoes:
- Pour in the chicken broth and add diced tomatoes. Bring the mixture to a simmer.

Simmer:
- Reduce the heat to low, cover the tagine or pot, and let it simmer for about 45 minutes to 1 hour, or until the chicken is tender and cooked through.

Add Apricots and Almonds:

- About 15 minutes before the end of cooking, add halved dried apricots and toasted almonds to the tagine. Allow them to absorb the flavors.

Check Seasoning:
- Taste the tagine and adjust the seasoning if necessary. You can add more salt, pepper, or any of the spices to suit your taste.

Garnish and Serve:
- Garnish the Moroccan Chicken Tagine with fresh cilantro or parsley just before serving. Serve it hot over couscous or with crusty bread.

Moroccan Tagine variations can include lamb, beef, fish, or a combination of meats. Vegetables like carrots, zucchini, and eggplant are also commonly used. The slow-cooking process in the tagine pot allows the flavors to meld together, creating a delicious and aromatic dish that is quintessentially Moroccan.

Shawarma (North Africa)

Ingredients:

For the Marinade:

- 1.5 kg boneless, skinless chicken thighs
- 1 cup plain yogurt
- 4 cloves garlic, minced
- 2 teaspoons ground cumin
- 2 teaspoons ground paprika
- 1 teaspoon ground turmeric
- 1 teaspoon ground coriander
- 1 teaspoon ground cinnamon
- Salt and pepper to taste
- 1/4 cup olive oil
- Juice of 1 lemon

For Serving:

- Flatbreads or pita
- Sliced tomatoes
- Sliced cucumbers
- Sliced red onions
- Fresh parsley or cilantro, chopped
- Tahini sauce or garlic sauce

Instructions:

Prepare the Marinade:
- In a bowl, combine yogurt, minced garlic, ground cumin, ground paprika, ground turmeric, ground coriander, ground cinnamon, salt, pepper, olive oil, and lemon juice. Mix well to create a smooth marinade.

Marinate the Chicken:
- Cut the chicken thighs into thin strips. Place them in the marinade, ensuring each piece is well-coated. Cover and refrigerate for at least 2 hours, or overnight for best results.

Preheat Oven:
- Preheat your oven to a high broil setting.

Thread Chicken onto Skewers:

- Thread the marinated chicken strips onto skewers, arranging them in a way that allows them to cook evenly.

Cook the Chicken:
- Place the skewers on a baking sheet and cook in the preheated oven for about 15-20 minutes, turning occasionally, until the chicken is cooked through and slightly charred.

Slice the Meat:
- Once cooked, remove the chicken from the skewers and thinly slice it.

Prepare Serving Ingredients:
- Warm the flatbreads or pitas. Prepare sliced tomatoes, cucumbers, red onions, and chopped parsley or cilantro.

Assemble Shawarma Wraps:
- Lay out the flatbreads or pitas. Place slices of the cooked chicken on top. Add the sliced vegetables and herbs. Drizzle with tahini sauce or garlic sauce.

Wrap and Serve:
- Roll the flatbreads or pitas to form wraps, enclosing the shawarma ingredients. Serve immediately.

Chicken Shawarma is customizable, and you can add your favorite toppings and sauces. It's a delicious and convenient meal that captures the essence of street food enjoyed in North African regions.

Bobo de Camarao (Mozambique)

Ingredients:

- 500g large shrimp, peeled and deveined
- 2 tablespoons lime or lemon juice
- Salt and pepper to taste
- 2 tablespoons olive oil
- 1 onion, finely chopped
- 3 cloves garlic, minced
- 1 red bell pepper, diced
- 1 green bell pepper, diced
- 1 tomato, diced
- 2 tablespoons tomato paste
- 1 can (400ml) coconut milk
- 1 cup yuca (cassava), peeled and grated
- 1 cup chicken or vegetable broth
- 1 teaspoon ground cumin
- 1 teaspoon ground coriander
- 1 teaspoon paprika
- Fresh cilantro or parsley for garnish
- Cooked white rice for serving

Instructions:

Marinate Shrimp:
- In a bowl, combine the peeled and deveined shrimp with lime or lemon juice, salt, and pepper. Let it marinate for about 15-20 minutes.

Sauté Vegetables:
- Heat olive oil in a large pot over medium heat. Add chopped onions and sauté until softened. Add minced garlic and continue sautéing until fragrant.

Add Bell Peppers and Tomato:
- Add diced red and green bell peppers and diced tomato to the pot. Cook for a few minutes until the vegetables are slightly tender.

Incorporate Tomato Paste:
- Stir in the tomato paste and cook for an additional 2-3 minutes.

Cook Shrimp:
- Add the marinated shrimp to the pot and cook until they turn pink and opaque.

Prepare Coconut Sauce:
- Pour in the coconut milk, grated yuca, and chicken or vegetable broth. Stir well to combine.

Season with Spices:
- Season the mixture with ground cumin, ground coriander, and paprika. Adjust salt and pepper to taste. Bring the mixture to a simmer.

Simmer:
- Let the Bobó de Camarão simmer for about 15-20 minutes, allowing the flavors to meld and the yuca to thicken the sauce.

Check Consistency:
- Check the consistency of the sauce. If it's too thick, you can add more broth to achieve the desired thickness.

Garnish and Serve:
- Garnish the Bobó de Camarão with fresh cilantro or parsley. Serve the dish hot over cooked white rice.

Bobó de Camarão is a delightful combination of shrimp, vegetables, and the creamy texture of coconut and yuca. It's often enjoyed as a main course, and the rich flavors make it a beloved dish in Mozambique.

Acheke (Ivory Coast)

Ingredients:

- 2 cups attiéké (fermented cassava couscous)
- 1 cup boiling water
- 2 tablespoons vegetable oil
- Salt to taste

Instructions:

Prepare the Attiéké:
- Place the attiéké in a large bowl.

Steam or Rehydrate:
- Pour the boiling water over the attiéké, making sure to distribute it evenly. Allow the attiéké to absorb the water for about 5 minutes.

Fluff the Attiéké:
- Using a fork, fluff the attiéké gently to separate the grains. Be careful not to mash or compress the attiéké.

Steam (Optional):
- If you prefer a softer texture, you can transfer the fluffed attiéké to a steamer and steam it for an additional 5-10 minutes. This step is optional, as some people prefer the traditional light and fluffy texture without steaming.

Season:
- Drizzle the attiéké with vegetable oil and sprinkle with salt. Gently toss to evenly distribute the oil and salt.

Serve:
- Acheke is ready to be served. It is often enjoyed as a side dish with grilled fish, meat, or stews.

Acheke is versatile and can be customized to suit different preferences. It is a common accompaniment to various Ivorian dishes and is loved for its unique taste and texture.

Kelewele (Ghana)

Ingredients:

- 4 ripe plantains
- 1 tablespoon grated fresh ginger
- 1 teaspoon ground cayenne pepper (adjust to taste)
- 1 teaspoon ground cinnamon
- 1 teaspoon ground cloves
- Salt to taste
- Vegetable oil for frying

Instructions:

Peel and Cut Plantains:
- Peel the ripe plantains and cut them into bite-sized chunks. You can cut them into rounds or cubes, depending on your preference.

Prepare Spices:
- In a bowl, combine grated fresh ginger, ground cayenne pepper, ground cinnamon, ground cloves, and salt. Mix the spices well.

Coat Plantains:
- Toss the plantain chunks in the spice mixture, ensuring that each piece is well-coated. You can use your hands to massage the spices onto the plantains.

Marinate:
- Let the spiced plantains marinate for at least 30 minutes to allow the flavors to infuse.

Heat Oil:
- In a deep pan or skillet, heat enough vegetable oil for frying over medium heat.

Fry Kelewele:
- Once the oil is hot, carefully add the spiced plantain chunks in batches. Fry until they are golden brown and crispy, turning occasionally to ensure even cooking.

Drain Excess Oil:
- Use a slotted spoon to remove the fried Kelewele from the oil and place them on a paper towel-lined plate to drain excess oil.

Serve:

- Kelewele is best served hot and can be enjoyed on its own as a snack or served as a side dish with a dip, such as spicy pepper sauce or groundnut (peanut) sauce.

Kelewele is a delightful street food in Ghana, often enjoyed for its unique combination of sweet, spicy, and savory flavors. It's a great way to experience the diverse and delicious tastes of Ghanaian cuisine.

Brik (Tunisia)

Ingredients:

- 8 sheets of thin pastry dough (known as warka or spring roll wrappers)
- 4 large eggs
- 1 can (about 150g) tuna, drained
- 2 tablespoons capers, chopped
- 2 tablespoons fresh parsley, chopped
- 1 teaspoon harissa (Tunisian hot chili paste), optional
- Salt and pepper to taste
- Vegetable oil for frying

Instructions:

Prepare Filling:
- In a bowl, combine the drained tuna, chopped capers, chopped parsley, and harissa (if using). Mix well. Season with salt and pepper to taste.

Prepare Pastry Sheets:
- Lay out the thin pastry sheets on a clean surface. If using spring roll wrappers, they can be cut into squares.

Assemble Brik:
- Place a spoonful of the tuna mixture in the center of each pastry sheet, creating a well in the center. Crack an egg into the well.

Fold and Seal:
- Fold the pastry over the filling to create a triangular or square shape. Seal the edges by pressing them together, ensuring the filling is enclosed.

Fry Brik:
- Heat vegetable oil in a deep fryer or a large, deep pan to around 350°F (180°C). Carefully place the filled and sealed briks into the hot oil, a few at a time.

Fry Until Golden:
- Fry the briks until they are golden brown and crispy, turning them to ensure even cooking. This usually takes 2-3 minutes per side.

Drain Excess Oil:
- Use a slotted spoon to remove the fried briks from the oil and place them on a paper towel-lined plate to drain any excess oil.

Serve:
- Serve the briks hot as a snack or appetizer. They can be enjoyed on their own or with a side of lemon wedges or your favorite dipping sauce.

Brik is known for its crispy exterior and the contrast between the crunchy pastry and the soft, runny egg inside. The combination of flavors from the tuna, capers, and parsley makes it a delicious and distinctive Tunisian treat.

Muamba de Galinha (Angola)

Ingredients:

- 1 whole chicken, cut into pieces
- 2 tablespoons palm oil
- 2 large onions, finely chopped
- 4 cloves garlic, minced
- 2 tomatoes, diced
- 2 red bell peppers, chopped
- 2 green bell peppers, chopped
- 2 cups chicken broth
- 1 cup coconut milk
- 2 bay leaves
- 1 tablespoon ground ginger
- 1 tablespoon ground paprika
- 1 tablespoon ground coriander
- 1 teaspoon ground cayenne pepper (adjust to taste)
- Salt and pepper to taste
- Fresh cilantro or parsley for garnish

Instructions:

Prepare Chicken:
- Cut the chicken into pieces and season them with salt, pepper, ground ginger, ground paprika, and ground coriander. Allow the chicken to marinate for at least 30 minutes.

Sauté Onions and Garlic:
- In a large pot, heat palm oil over medium heat. Add finely chopped onions and minced garlic. Sauté until the onions are translucent.

Brown Chicken:
- Add the marinated chicken to the pot and brown it on all sides.

Add Vegetables:
- Stir in diced tomatoes, chopped red and green bell peppers. Cook for a few minutes until the vegetables begin to soften.

Incorporate Spices:
- Add bay leaves and ground cayenne pepper to the pot. Mix well to incorporate the spices.

Pour in Liquids:
- Pour in chicken broth and coconut milk. Bring the mixture to a simmer.

Simmer:
- Reduce the heat to low, cover the pot, and let the Muamba de Galinha simmer for about 45 minutes to 1 hour, or until the chicken is tender and cooked through.

Adjust Seasoning:
- Taste the stew and adjust the seasoning with salt and pepper if needed. You can also adjust the level of spiciness according to your preference.

Garnish and Serve:
- Garnish the Muamba de Galinha with fresh cilantro or parsley before serving. Serve it hot over rice or with funge.

Muamba de Galinha is a dish that captures the essence of Angolan cuisine, combining the rich flavors of spices, palm oil, and coconut milk. It's a comforting and aromatic stew that is often enjoyed during festive occasions and gatherings in Angola.

Mafé (Senegal)

Ingredients:

- 1.5 lbs (700g) beef or lamb, cut into stew-sized pieces
- 1 cup peanut butter (unsweetened and natural)
- 2 large onions, finely chopped
- 3 tomatoes, diced
- 2 sweet potatoes, peeled and diced
- 2 carrots, peeled and sliced
- 1 eggplant, diced
- 1 bell pepper, diced
- 3 cloves garlic, minced
- 2 tablespoons tomato paste
- 1/4 cup vegetable oil
- 4 cups beef or vegetable broth
- 1 teaspoon ground cayenne pepper (adjust to taste)
- Salt and pepper to taste
- Fresh cilantro for garnish
- Cooked rice or couscous for serving

Instructions:

Brown the Meat:
- In a large pot, heat vegetable oil over medium-high heat. Brown the meat on all sides. Remove the meat from the pot and set it aside.

Sauté Onions and Garlic:
- In the same pot, add chopped onions and minced garlic. Sauté until the onions are softened and translucent.

Add Tomato Paste:
- Stir in the tomato paste and cook for a couple of minutes until it becomes fragrant.

Prepare Peanut Sauce:
- Add peanut butter to the pot, along with diced tomatoes. Stir well to combine the peanut butter and tomatoes.

Add Meat and Broth:
- Return the browned meat to the pot. Pour in the broth, stirring to incorporate the ingredients.

Simmer:

- Allow the mixture to simmer over medium heat for about 30 minutes, stirring occasionally.

Add Vegetables:
- Add diced sweet potatoes, sliced carrots, diced eggplant, and diced bell pepper to the pot. Mix well.

Season and Continue Cooking:
- Season the stew with ground cayenne pepper, salt, and pepper. Continue cooking until the vegetables are tender and the meat is cooked through, usually another 20-30 minutes.

Check and Adjust:
- Taste the Mafé and adjust the seasoning if necessary. Add more salt, pepper, or cayenne pepper according to your preference.

Serve:
- Garnish the Mafé with fresh cilantro and serve it hot over cooked rice or couscous.

Mafé is a comforting and hearty dish with a rich and nutty flavor from the peanuts. It's a beloved dish in Senegal and across West Africa, often enjoyed during family meals and special occasions.

Samosa (North Africa)

Ingredients:

For the Filling:

- 2 large potatoes, boiled and diced
- 1 cup green peas (fresh or frozen)
- 1 large onion, finely chopped
- 2 cloves garlic, minced
- 1 teaspoon grated ginger
- 1 teaspoon ground cumin
- 1 teaspoon ground coriander
- 1/2 teaspoon turmeric
- 1/2 teaspoon ground cinnamon
- 1/2 teaspoon cayenne pepper (adjust to taste)
- Salt and pepper to taste
- 2 tablespoons vegetable oil
- Fresh cilantro or parsley, chopped

For the Samosa Dough:

- 2 cups all-purpose flour
- 1/4 cup vegetable oil
- Water for kneading
- Pinch of salt

For Frying:

- Vegetable oil for deep frying

Instructions:

Prepare the Filling:

> In a pan, heat vegetable oil over medium heat. Add chopped onions and sauté until translucent.
> Add minced garlic and grated ginger to the onions. Sauté for another minute until fragrant.
> Add ground cumin, ground coriander, turmeric, ground cinnamon, cayenne pepper, salt, and pepper. Stir well to combine the spices.

Add diced boiled potatoes and green peas to the spice mixture. Mix thoroughly and cook for a few minutes until the vegetables are well-coated with the spices. Stir in fresh cilantro or parsley and cook for an additional minute. Remove the filling from heat and let it cool.

Prepare the Samosa Dough:

In a mixing bowl, combine all-purpose flour, vegetable oil, and a pinch of salt. Gradually add water and knead the mixture to form a smooth and firm dough. Cover the dough with a damp cloth and let it rest for about 30 minutes.

Assemble and Fry the Samosas:

Divide the dough into small balls and roll each ball into a thin, oval-shaped sheet.
Cut the oval sheet in half to create two semi-circles.
Take one semi-circle and fold it into a cone shape, sealing the edges with a little water.
Fill the cone with the prepared vegetable filling.
Seal the open edge of the cone to form a triangular samosa. Repeat the process for the remaining dough and filling.
Heat vegetable oil in a deep frying pan over medium heat.
Once the oil is hot, carefully place the prepared samosas into the oil, a few at a time.
Fry the samosas until they are golden brown and crispy, turning them to ensure even cooking.
Use a slotted spoon to remove the fried samosas from the oil and place them on a paper towel-lined plate to drain excess oil.
Serve the samosas hot with your favorite dipping sauce or chutney.

North African-style samosas offer a delicious blend of flavors and spices, making them a popular snack enjoyed across the region. They are often served during celebrations, festivals, and family gatherings.

Pap en Vleis/Shisa Nyama (South Africa)

Pap (Maize Porridge):

Ingredients:

- 2 cups maize meal (cornmeal)
- 4 cups water
- Salt to taste

Instructions:

Boil Water:
- In a pot, bring 4 cups of water to a boil.

Add Maize Meal:
- Gradually add maize meal to the boiling water, stirring continuously to prevent lumps from forming.

Cook Pap:
- Reduce the heat to low, cover the pot, and let the maize meal simmer for about 30 minutes. Stir occasionally to ensure even cooking.

Season:
- Add salt to taste and continue cooking until the pap reaches a smooth and thick consistency.

Serve:
- Remove the pot from heat and let the pap rest for a few minutes. Serve it hot.

Vleis (Grilled Meat):

Ingredients:

- Assorted meats such as beef steaks, lamb chops, sausages, or chicken
- Marinade (optional)
- Salt and pepper to taste

Instructions:

Prepare the Grill:
- If using a barbecue or grill, preheat it to a medium-high heat.

Season the Meat:

- Season the assorted meats with salt and pepper. You can also marinate them in your favorite marinade for added flavor.

Grill the Meat:
- Grill the meat on the barbecue or grill until it reaches your desired level of doneness. Turn the meat occasionally to ensure even cooking.

Rest and Serve:
- Let the grilled meat rest for a few minutes before serving.

Serving "Pap en Vleis/Shisa Nyama":

Plating:
- Serve a portion of pap on each plate.

Top with Grilled Meat:
- Arrange the grilled meat on top of the pap.

Sauce or Relish (Optional):
- Serve with a flavorful sauce or relish on the side, such as chakalaka or tomato and onion relish.

Enjoy:
- "Pap en Vleis/Shisa Nyama" is ready to be enjoyed. Eat with your hands or utensils, depending on preference.

This dish is not only a culinary delight but also a cultural experience, reflecting the rich diversity and traditions of South African cuisine. It is often enjoyed in a communal setting, bringing people together to share good food and company.

Chermoula (North Africa)

Ingredients:

- 1 cup fresh cilantro, chopped
- 1 cup fresh parsley, chopped
- 3 cloves garlic, minced
- 1 teaspoon ground cumin
- 1 teaspoon ground coriander
- 1 teaspoon paprika
- 1/2 teaspoon cayenne pepper (adjust to taste)
- Zest and juice of 1 lemon
- 1/4 cup extra-virgin olive oil
- Salt and pepper to taste

Instructions:

Combine Herbs:
- In a food processor or blender, combine chopped cilantro and parsley.

Add Aromatics:
- Add minced garlic, ground cumin, ground coriander, paprika, and cayenne pepper to the herbs.

Add Lemon Zest and Juice:
- Grate the zest of one lemon and squeeze its juice. Add both to the mixture.

Blend:
- Pulse or blend the ingredients until you get a coarse paste. You can adjust the consistency by adding more olive oil if needed.

Season:
- Season the chermoula with salt and pepper to taste. Adjust the level of cayenne pepper for spiciness according to your preference.

Add Olive Oil:
- With the blender or food processor running, slowly drizzle in the extra-virgin olive oil. Continue blending until the chermoula reaches a smooth and well-emulsified consistency.

Taste and Adjust:
- Taste the chermoula and adjust the seasoning if necessary. You can add more salt, pepper, or lemon juice to balance the flavors.

Marinate or Serve:

- Use the chermoula as a marinade for fish, chicken, or vegetables before grilling or roasting. Alternatively, it can be served as a sauce or condiment alongside grilled dishes.

Chermoula adds a burst of fresh and zesty flavors to dishes, and its aromatic profile enhances the overall culinary experience. It's a staple in North African cuisine and a fantastic way to infuse depth and vibrancy into various meals.

Domoda (Gambia)

Ingredients:

For the Peanut Sauce:

- 1 cup peanut butter (unsweetened and natural)
- 1 large onion, finely chopped
- 3 tomatoes, diced
- 2 tablespoons tomato paste
- 2 tablespoons vegetable oil
- 3 cloves garlic, minced
- 1 teaspoon ground cayenne pepper (adjust to taste)
- 1 teaspoon ground paprika
- 1 teaspoon ground coriander
- Salt and pepper to taste
- 4 cups chicken broth
- 1 cup okra, sliced (optional)
- 1 medium eggplant, diced
- 2 carrots, peeled and sliced
- 1 sweet potato, peeled and diced

For the Chicken:

- 1 whole chicken, cut into pieces
- 1 lemon, juiced
- Salt and pepper to taste

For Serving:

- Cooked rice

Instructions:

Prepare the Chicken:

Marinate Chicken:
- In a bowl, season the chicken pieces with lemon juice, salt, and pepper. Let it marinate for at least 30 minutes.

Cook Chicken:

- In a large pot, heat vegetable oil over medium-high heat. Brown the marinated chicken pieces on all sides. Remove the chicken and set it aside.

Prepare the Peanut Sauce:

Sauté Vegetables:
- In the same pot, add chopped onions and minced garlic. Sauté until the onions are translucent.

Add Tomatoes and Spices:
- Add diced tomatoes, tomato paste, ground cayenne pepper, ground paprika, ground coriander, salt, and pepper. Stir well to combine.

Incorporate Peanut Butter:
- Add peanut butter to the pot and mix it with the tomato mixture until well combined.

Pour in Chicken Broth:
- Gradually pour in the chicken broth while stirring to create a smooth sauce.

Add Vegetables:
- Return the browned chicken to the pot. Add sliced okra (if using), diced eggplant, sliced carrots, and diced sweet potato.

Simmer:
- Let the Domoda simmer over medium-low heat for about 30-40 minutes or until the vegetables are tender and the chicken is cooked through.

Adjust Seasoning:
- Taste and adjust the seasoning if necessary. You can add more salt, pepper, or spices to suit your taste.

Serve:
- Serve the Domoda hot over cooked rice.

Domoda is a delicious and comforting dish that showcases the unique flavors of Gambian cuisine. The combination of the savory peanut sauce and the tender chicken, along with the assortment of vegetables, makes it a hearty and satisfying meal.

Bambara Beans Soup (Nigeria)

Ingredients:

- 2 cups Bambara beans
- 1 cup crayfish, ground
- 1 cup periwinkle (optional)
- 1 cup ugba (ukpaka) - oil bean
- 2 tablespoons powdered potash (food tenderizer)
- 2 cubes of seasoning (Maggi or Knorr)
- 2 teaspoons ground pepper (adjust to taste)
- Salt to taste
- 1 cup palm oil
- Water
- Vegetables (ugu, spinach, or any leafy green), chopped

Instructions:

Prepare the Bambara Beans:
- Soak the Bambara beans in water for about 5-6 hours or overnight.

Peel the Bambara Beans:
- After soaking, peel off the skin from the beans. You can use your fingers or a mortar and pestle to facilitate the peeling process.

Blend the Beans:
- Rinse the peeled beans and blend them into a smooth paste using a blender or food processor. Add water as needed to achieve a smooth consistency.

Extract the Milk:
- Use a sieve or cheesecloth to extract the milk from the blended beans. Add water and strain until you extract all the milk.

Prepare Potash Solution:
- Dissolve the powdered potash in water and sieve out the water. Set the potash solution aside.

Cook the Bambara Bean Paste:
- In a pot, cook the Bambara bean paste over medium heat, stirring constantly. As it cooks, it thickens and becomes more elastic.

Add Palm Oil:
- Add palm oil to the cooking Bambara bean paste. Continue stirring.

Add Potash Solution:

- Pour in the potash solution and continue stirring until the mixture is well combined.

Season and Add Crayfish:
- Add seasoning cubes, ground pepper, and ground crayfish. Stir to incorporate the seasonings.

Cook the Soup:
- Add water to achieve your desired soup consistency. Stir well and let the soup cook over medium heat.

Add Periwinkle and Ugba:
- If using periwinkle and ugba, add them to the soup. Stir and continue cooking.

Season to Taste:
- Season the soup with salt and adjust the seasonings to your taste.

Add Vegetables:
- Finally, add the chopped vegetables (ugu, spinach, or any leafy green). Stir well and cook until the vegetables are tender.

Serve:
- Once the soup is cooked to your satisfaction, remove it from heat. It is now ready to be served.

Bambara Beans Soup is often enjoyed with a side of fufu, rice, or any other preferred accompaniment. The nutty flavor of Bambara beans, combined with the richness of palm oil and other ingredients, makes this soup a unique and tasty dish in Nigerian cuisine.

Berbere Chicken (Eritrea)

Ingredients:

For the Berbere Spice Blend:

- 2 tablespoons paprika
- 1 tablespoon cayenne pepper (adjust to taste)
- 1 tablespoon ground cumin
- 1 tablespoon ground coriander
- 1 tablespoon ground cardamom
- 1 tablespoon ground fenugreek
- 1 tablespoon ground ginger
- 1 tablespoon ground cinnamon
- 1 teaspoon ground cloves
- 1 teaspoon ground allspice
- 1 teaspoon ground nutmeg
- 1 teaspoon black pepper
- 1 teaspoon salt

For the Berbere Chicken:

- 4 bone-in, skin-on chicken thighs
- 2 tablespoons vegetable oil
- 1 large onion, finely chopped
- 3 cloves garlic, minced
- 1 tablespoon grated fresh ginger
- 2 tablespoons berbere spice blend (adjust to taste)
- 1 can (14 oz) diced tomatoes
- 1 cup chicken broth
- Salt to taste
- Fresh cilantro or parsley for garnish

Instructions:

Prepare the Berbere Spice Blend:

- Combine Spices:
    - In a bowl, combine all the spices for the berbere spice blend. Mix well to create a homogenous spice mixture.

Prepare the Berbere Chicken:

Season Chicken:
- Rub the chicken thighs with 1-2 tablespoons of the berbere spice blend, ensuring they are well-coated. Let them marinate for at least 30 minutes.

Sear Chicken:
- In a large, oven-safe skillet, heat vegetable oil over medium-high heat. Sear the chicken thighs on both sides until they develop a golden-brown crust. Remove the chicken from the skillet and set it aside.

Sauté Onion, Garlic, and Ginger:
- In the same skillet, add finely chopped onion. Sauté until the onion becomes translucent. Add minced garlic and grated ginger, and continue to sauté for an additional 1-2 minutes.

Add Berbere Spice Blend:
- Stir in 2 tablespoons of the berbere spice blend (adjust according to your spice preference) and cook for a couple of minutes to toast the spices.

Incorporate Tomatoes and Broth:
- Add diced tomatoes and chicken broth to the skillet. Stir well to combine.

Return Chicken to Skillet:
- Return the seared chicken thighs to the skillet, nestling them into the sauce.

Simmer and Cook:
- Reduce the heat to low, cover the skillet, and let the chicken simmer in the sauce for about 25-30 minutes or until the chicken is cooked through.

Check and Adjust Seasoning:
- Taste the sauce and adjust the seasoning with salt and additional berbere spice blend if desired.

Finish in the Oven (Optional):
- If you prefer, you can finish cooking the chicken in a preheated oven at 375°F (190°C) for an additional 15-20 minutes until the skin is crispy.

Garnish and Serve:
- Garnish the Berbere Chicken with fresh cilantro or parsley. Serve it hot, either over rice, injera (traditional Ethiopian flatbread), or with your preferred side.

Berbere Chicken is a bold and aromatic dish that showcases the unique flavors of the berbere spice blend. The combination of spices, tomatoes, and chicken creates a delicious and satisfying meal that reflects the rich culinary heritage of Eritrea.

Atayef (North Africa)

Ingredients:

For the Atayef Pancakes:

- 2 cups all-purpose flour
- 2 tablespoons semolina
- 1 tablespoon sugar
- 1 teaspoon baking powder
- 1/2 teaspoon instant yeast
- 2 cups warm water

For the Nut Filling:

- 1 cup mixed nuts (walnuts, almonds, pistachios), finely chopped
- 1/2 cup sugar
- 1 teaspoon ground cinnamon
- 1-2 tablespoons orange blossom water or rose water (optional)

For the Cheese Filling (Alternative):

- 1 cup ricotta cheese or unsalted white cheese
- 2 tablespoons sugar
- 1 teaspoon orange blossom water or rose water (optional)

For Frying:

- Vegetable oil for frying

For Serving:

- Powdered sugar for dusting

Instructions:

Prepare the Atayef Pancakes:

    Mix Dry Ingredients:
- In a bowl, whisk together the flour, semolina, sugar, baking powder, and instant yeast.

    Add Water:

- Gradually add the warm water to the dry ingredients, whisking continuously to form a smooth batter. The batter should have a pouring consistency, similar to pancake batter. Let it rest for 15-20 minutes.

Cook Pancakes:
- Heat a non-stick skillet or griddle over medium heat. Pour small portions of the batter to form small pancakes (about 3 inches in diameter). Cook only on one side until bubbles form on the surface and the edges start to lift. The pancakes should not be flipped.

Remove and Cool:
- Remove the pancakes from the skillet and let them cool. They will have a smooth side and a side with small bubbles.

Prepare the Nut Filling:

Mix Ingredients:
- In a bowl, combine the chopped nuts, sugar, ground cinnamon, and orange blossom water or rose water (if using). Mix well to create the nut filling.

Prepare the Cheese Filling (Alternative):

Combine Ingredients:
- In another bowl, mix the ricotta or white cheese with sugar and orange blossom water or rose water (if using) to create the cheese filling.

Assemble and Fold Atayef:

Fill the Pancakes:
- Place a tablespoon of the desired filling (nut or cheese) on the side of the pancake with bubbles.

Fold and Seal:
- Fold the pancake in half to form a half-moon shape. Pinch the edges to seal the filling inside.

Optional Second Fold:
- For a different presentation, you can fold the sealed edge again to form a triangle.

Repeat:
- Repeat the process until all pancakes are filled and folded.

Fry Atayef:

Heat Oil:
- In a deep pan, heat vegetable oil over medium heat for frying.

Fry Until Golden:

- Carefully place the filled and folded Atayef in the hot oil and fry until they are golden brown on both sides. Use a slotted spoon to remove them from the oil.

Drain Excess Oil:
- Place the fried Atayef on paper towels to drain excess oil.

Serve:

Dust with Powdered Sugar:
- Once the Atayef have cooled slightly, dust them with powdered sugar.

Serve Warm:
- Atayef is best enjoyed warm. They can be served as is or with a side of simple syrup for extra sweetness.

Atayef is a delightful dessert that brings joy to special occasions, especially during Ramadan. The combination of the soft pancake and the flavorful filling makes it a beloved treat in North African and Middle Eastern cuisines.

Efo Riro (Nigeria)

Ingredients:

For the Stew Base:

- 4 cups spinach or other leafy greens, chopped
- 2 cups tomatoes, blended
- 1 cup red bell peppers, blended
- 1 cup onions, finely chopped
- 1/2 cup palm oil
- 3 tablespoons ground crayfish
- 2 tablespoons locust beans (iru) or ogiri (fermented locust beans) - optional
- 2 stock cubes (Maggi or Knorr)
- Salt and pepper to taste

Assorted Meats and Fish:

- 1/2 lb goat meat, cut into bite-sized pieces
- 1/2 lb cow tripe (shaki), cleaned and cut into strips
- 1/2 lb beef, cut into bite-sized pieces
- 1/2 lb stockfish, pre-soaked and cut into chunks
- 1/2 cup dried fish, deboned and flaked
- 1/2 cup cooked and shredded or smoked fish

Additional Ingredients:

- 2 tablespoons ground crayfish
- 2 tablespoons locust beans (iru) or ogiri (fermented locust beans) - optional
- 1 cup water or stock (adjust as needed)

Instructions:

Prepare the Assorted Meats and Fish:

Cook Meat and Tripe:
- In a pot, cook the goat meat, cow tripe, and beef with seasoning cubes until tender. You can use a pressure cooker to expedite the cooking process.

Soak Stockfish:

- Pre-soak the stockfish in warm water until it softens. Clean and cut it into chunks.

Debone and Flake Dried Fish:
- Debone and flake the dried fish if it's not already done. Remove any bones and set aside.

Prepare the Stew Base:

Heat Palm Oil:
- In a large pot, heat the palm oil until it becomes clear. Be careful not to overheat it.

Sauté Onions:
- Add the finely chopped onions to the heated palm oil and sauté until the onions are translucent.

Blend Tomatoes and Peppers:
- Blend the tomatoes and red bell peppers until smooth.

Add Blended Tomatoes and Peppers:
- Pour the blended mixture into the pot with sautéed onions. Stir well and let it cook until the liquid reduces, and the oil begins to separate from the mixture.

Add Locust Beans and Ground Crayfish:
- Add locust beans (iru or ogiri) and ground crayfish to the pot. Stir to combine.

Add Cooked Assorted Meats and Fish:
- Add the cooked meats and fish to the pot. Stir well to combine them with the stew base.

Add Water or Stock:
- Pour in water or stock to achieve your desired consistency. Adjust the seasoning with salt and pepper to taste.

Simmer:
- Let the stew simmer for about 15-20 minutes to allow the flavors to meld and the stew to thicken.

Add Chopped Spinach:
- Add the chopped spinach or leafy greens to the pot. Stir well and let it cook until the greens are wilted.

Check and Adjust:
- Taste the Efo Riro and adjust the seasoning if necessary. If you prefer a spicier stew, you can add more pepper.

Serve:

- Efo Riro is ready to be served. It is often enjoyed with rice, pounded yam, fufu, or any preferred Nigerian staple.

Efo Riro is a flavorful and hearty stew that showcases the diversity and richness of Nigerian cuisine. It's a comforting dish that is often served during celebrations and family gatherings.

Kushari (Egypt)

Ingredients:

For the Rice and Lentils:

- 1 cup dried brown lentils, rinsed
- 1 cup white rice
- 4 cups water
- Salt to taste

For the Macaroni and Chickpeas:

- 1 cup macaroni pasta
- 1 cup canned chickpeas, drained and rinsed
- Salt to taste

For the Tomato Sauce:

- 2 tablespoons vegetable oil
- 1 onion, finely chopped
- 3 cloves garlic, minced
- 2 cups canned crushed tomatoes
- 1 teaspoon ground cumin
- 1 teaspoon ground coriander
- 1/2 teaspoon cayenne pepper (optional)
- Salt and pepper to taste

For the Fried Onions:

- Vegetable oil for frying
- 1 large onion, thinly sliced

For Serving:

- White vinegar
- Garlic sauce (optional)

Instructions:

Prepare the Rice and Lentils:

    Cook Lentils:

- In a pot, combine rinsed brown lentils with water. Bring to a boil, then reduce the heat and simmer until the lentils are tender. Add salt to taste.

Cook Rice:
- In a separate pot, rinse white rice and cook it in water until tender. Add salt to taste.

Prepare the Macaroni and Chickpeas:

Cook Macaroni:
- Cook the macaroni according to the package instructions until al dente. Drain and set aside.

Prepare Chickpeas:
- In a pot, heat the canned chickpeas with some salt until warmed through.

Prepare the Tomato Sauce:

Sauté Onion and Garlic:
- In a saucepan, heat vegetable oil. Sauté chopped onion and minced garlic until softened.

Add Crushed Tomatoes:
- Add crushed tomatoes to the saucepan and bring the mixture to a simmer.

Season the Sauce:
- Add ground cumin, ground coriander, cayenne pepper (if using), salt, and pepper to the sauce. Simmer for about 15-20 minutes, allowing the flavors to meld.

Prepare the Fried Onions:

Fry Onions:
- Heat vegetable oil in a pan. Fry thinly sliced onions until they become golden and crispy. Remove them from the oil and let them drain on a paper towel.

Assemble Kushari:

Layer Ingredients:
- In individual serving bowls or on a large serving platter, layer the cooked rice, lentils, macaroni, and chickpeas.

Top with Tomato Sauce:
- Pour the spiced tomato sauce over the layered ingredients.

Garnish with Fried Onions:

- Garnish the Kushari with the crispy fried onions.

Serve with Condiments:
- Serve the Kushari with white vinegar on the side for drizzling. Optionally, you can also serve it with garlic sauce.

Mix and Enjoy:
- Before eating, mix the layers together to combine all the flavors. The combination of textures and the spiced tomato sauce creates a delicious and satisfying dish.

Kushari is a beloved street food in Egypt, enjoyed by locals and visitors alike. Its humble yet flavorful ingredients make it a comforting and budget-friendly meal.

Dibi (Senegal)

Ingredients:

For the Marinade:

- 2 lbs lamb chops (shoulder or rib chops)
- 1 large onion, finely chopped
- 3 cloves garlic, minced
- 1 tablespoon Dijon mustard
- 1 teaspoon ground black pepper
- 1 teaspoon paprika
- 1 teaspoon ground cayenne pepper (adjust to taste)
- 1 teaspoon ground ginger
- 1 teaspoon ground cumin
- 1 teaspoon thyme
- 1 teaspoon salt (or to taste)
- 1/4 cup vegetable oil
- Juice of 1 lemon
- Fresh parsley or cilantro for garnish (optional)

For Serving:

- Lemon wedges
- Grilled or steamed vegetables (optional)
- Sides like couscous or rice (optional)

Instructions:

Prepare the Marinade:

    Mix Ingredients:
- In a bowl, combine the finely chopped onion, minced garlic, Dijon mustard, black pepper, paprika, cayenne pepper, ground ginger, ground cumin, thyme, salt, vegetable oil, and lemon juice. Mix the ingredients well to form a paste.

    Marinate Lamb Chops:
- Place the lamb chops in a large bowl or shallow dish. Rub the marinade all over the lamb chops, ensuring they are well-coated. Cover the bowl or dish and let the lamb marinate for at least 2 hours or preferably overnight in the refrigerator.

Grill the Lamb Chops:

Preheat Grill:
- Preheat your grill to medium-high heat.

Remove Excess Marinade:
- Remove the lamb chops from the marinade, allowing any excess marinade to drip off.

Grill Lamb Chops:
- Place the lamb chops on the preheated grill. Grill for about 4-6 minutes per side, or until they reach your desired level of doneness. The cooking time may vary based on the thickness of the chops and your preferred doneness.

Baste with Marinade (Optional):
- Optionally, you can baste the lamb chops with a bit of the marinade during the grilling process to enhance the flavor.

Rest and Garnish:
- Once the lamb chops are grilled to perfection, remove them from the grill and let them rest for a few minutes. This allows the juices to redistribute.

Garnish:
- Garnish the grilled lamb chops with fresh parsley or cilantro if desired.

Serve:

Plate and Arrange:
- Arrange the grilled lamb chops on a serving platter.

Serving Suggestions:
- Serve the Dibi with lemon wedges on the side for squeezing over the meat. You can also serve it with grilled or steamed vegetables and your choice of sides like couscous or rice.

Enjoy:
- Dibi is ready to be enjoyed. Serve it hot and savor the delicious flavors of the grilled lamb.

Dibi is a delightful and savory dish that captures the essence of Senegalese cuisine. The combination of the aromatic marinade and the charred, grilled lamb chops makes it a favorite among those who appreciate bold and flavorful grilled meats.

Lentil Wat (Ethiopia)

Ingredients:

- 2 cups red lentils, washed and drained
- 1 large onion, finely chopped
- 3 cloves garlic, minced
- 1 tablespoon fresh ginger, minced
- 2 tablespoons berbere spice blend (adjust to taste)
- 1 teaspoon ground cumin
- 1 teaspoon ground coriander
- 1/2 teaspoon turmeric powder
- 1/4 cup vegetable oil
- 1 can (14 oz) diced tomatoes
- 4 cups vegetable broth or water
- Salt to taste
- Fresh cilantro or parsley for garnish (optional)

Instructions:

Prepare Lentils:
- Rinse the red lentils under cold water until the water runs clear. Drain and set aside.

Sauté Onion, Garlic, and Ginger:
- In a large pot, heat the vegetable oil over medium heat. Add the finely chopped onion and sauté until it becomes translucent. Add minced garlic and minced ginger, and continue to sauté for another 2-3 minutes.

Add Berbere Spice and Other Ground Spices:
- Add the berbere spice blend, ground cumin, ground coriander, and turmeric powder to the pot. Stir well to coat the onions in the spices.

Incorporate Lentils:
- Add the washed and drained red lentils to the pot. Stir to coat the lentils in the spice mixture.

Add Diced Tomatoes:
- Pour in the diced tomatoes (with their juice) into the pot. Mix well.

Pour in Broth or Water:
- Add the vegetable broth or water to the pot. Stir to combine all the ingredients.

Simmer:

- Bring the mixture to a boil, then reduce the heat to low, cover the pot, and let it simmer for about 20-25 minutes or until the lentils are tender.

Season with Salt:
- Once the lentils are cooked, season the Lentil Wat with salt to taste. Adjust the seasoning as needed.

Garnish (Optional):
- If desired, garnish the Lentil Wat with fresh cilantro or parsley for added freshness.

Serve:
- Lentil Wat is traditionally served with injera, but you can also enjoy it with rice, bread, or your preferred grain.

Lentil Wat is a delicious and nutritious dish that showcases the vibrant flavors of Ethiopian cuisine. The berbere spice blend, a key component of many Ethiopian dishes, adds a unique and aromatic touch to the stew. Enjoy the hearty and warming Lentil Wat as a satisfying meal on its own or as part of a larger Ethiopian feast.

Mango Curry Chicken (Mauritius)

Ingredients:

- 2 lbs chicken pieces (thighs, drumsticks, or a combination)
- 2 large ripe mangoes, peeled, pitted, and diced
- 1 large onion, finely chopped
- 3 cloves garlic, minced
- 1 tablespoon fresh ginger, minced
- 2 tablespoons curry powder
- 1 teaspoon turmeric powder
- 1 teaspoon cumin powder
- 1 teaspoon coriander powder
- 1/2 teaspoon chili powder (adjust to taste)
- 1 can (14 oz) coconut milk
- 1 cup chicken broth
- 2 tablespoons vegetable oil
- Salt and pepper to taste
- Fresh cilantro for garnish (optional)
- Cooked rice for serving

Instructions:

Prep Chicken:
- Season the chicken pieces with salt and pepper. Set aside.

Sauté Onion, Garlic, and Ginger:
- In a large pot or deep skillet, heat vegetable oil over medium heat. Add finely chopped onion and sauté until it becomes translucent. Add minced garlic and minced ginger, and continue to sauté for another 2-3 minutes.

Add Curry Spices:
- Add curry powder, turmeric powder, cumin powder, coriander powder, and chili powder to the pot. Stir well to coat the onions in the spice mixture.

Brown Chicken:
- Add the seasoned chicken pieces to the pot. Brown the chicken on all sides, ensuring it gets coated with the spices.

Incorporate Mango and Coconut Milk:
- Add the diced mangoes to the pot. Pour in the coconut milk and chicken broth. Stir to combine all the ingredients.

Simmer:

- Bring the mixture to a gentle boil, then reduce the heat to low. Cover the pot and let it simmer for about 25-30 minutes or until the chicken is cooked through and the flavors meld.

Check Seasoning:
- Taste the curry and adjust the seasoning with salt and pepper as needed. If you prefer a spicier curry, you can add more chili powder.

Garnish and Serve:
- Garnish the Mango Curry Chicken with fresh cilantro if desired. Serve the curry over cooked rice.

Enjoy:
- Mango Curry Chicken is now ready to be enjoyed. The combination of sweet mangoes and aromatic spices creates a delicious and unique flavor profile.

Mango Curry Chicken is a wonderful representation of the fusion of flavors found in Mauritian cuisine. The sweetness of mangoes balances the savory and spicy elements of the curry, creating a dish that is both comforting and exotic. Serve it with rice or your preferred side for a complete and satisfying meal.

Nsala Soup (Congo)

Ingredients:

For the Soup:

- 2 lbs catfish fillets (or any white fish)
- 2 large yams, peeled and cut into chunks
- 1 onion, finely chopped
- 3 cloves garlic, minced
- 1 tablespoon fresh ginger, minced
- 2 teaspoons ground pepper (adjust to taste)
- 2 teaspoons ground crayfish
- 2 tablespoons palm oil
- Salt to taste
- Water

For the Spice Blend:

- 2 teaspoons uziza seeds (substitute with black pepper if unavailable)
- 2 teaspoons calabash nutmeg (ehuru)
- 2 teaspoons utazi leaves, chopped (optional)
- 2 teaspoons scent leaves (nchanwu or basil), chopped (optional)

Instructions:

Prepare the Fish:

Clean and Cut Fish:
- Clean the catfish fillets thoroughly. Cut them into medium-sized chunks.

Marinate Fish:
- In a bowl, season the fish chunks with minced garlic, minced ginger, ground pepper, and salt. Let it marinate for at least 30 minutes.

Prepare the Spice Blend:

Grind Uziza Seeds and Calabash Nutmeg:
- In a spice grinder or mortar and pestle, grind uziza seeds and calabash nutmeg until you get a fine powder.

Chop Utazi and Scent Leaves:

- If using, chop utazi leaves and scent leaves (nchanwu or basil) finely. Set aside.

Cook the Soup:

Cook Yams:
- In a large pot, place the yam chunks and cover with water. Boil until the yams are tender. Once cooked, mash some of the yams to thicken the soup.

Prepare Spice Mixture:
- In a small bowl, mix the ground uziza seeds, ground calabash nutmeg, and, if using, chopped utazi and scent leaves.

Cook Fish:
- In the same pot with the yams, add the marinated fish chunks. Cook until the fish is almost done.

Add Spice Mixture:
- Add the prepared spice mixture to the pot. Stir gently to combine the spices with the fish.

Add Palm Oil:
- Pour in the palm oil and continue stirring. The palm oil adds richness and flavor to the soup.

Adjust Seasoning:
- Adjust the seasoning by adding more salt and ground crayfish to taste.

Simmer:
- Let the soup simmer for an additional 10-15 minutes, allowing the flavors to meld and the fish to cook through.

Check Consistency:
- If the soup is too thick, you can add more water to achieve your desired consistency.

Serve:
- Nsala Soup is now ready to be served. It is traditionally enjoyed with fufu or any preferred side.

Nsala Soup is known for its light color, rich taste, and aromatic flavors. The combination of spices and the use of catfish or white fish contribute to its unique and satisfying character. It's a comforting dish enjoyed in Congolese households and represents the diverse and delicious cuisine of the region.

Suya (Nigeria)

Ingredients:

For the Suya Spice Mix:

- 2 tablespoons ground peanuts (groundnut powder)
- 1 tablespoon ground cayenne pepper
- 1 tablespoon paprika
- 1 teaspoon onion powder
- 1 teaspoon garlic powder
- 1 teaspoon ginger powder
- 1 teaspoon ground white pepper
- 1 teaspoon bouillon powder or ground stock cube
- Salt to taste

For the Skewers:

- 2 lbs chicken breast or beef, thinly sliced
- Wooden skewers, soaked in water for at least 30 minutes

For Serving:

- Sliced onions
- Sliced tomatoes
- Sliced cucumber
- Spicy pepper sauce (optional)

Instructions:

Prepare the Suya Spice Mix:

> Roast Ground Peanuts:
> - In a dry pan over medium heat, roast the ground peanuts until they become fragrant and start to release their oils. Be careful not to burn them. Allow them to cool.
>
> Grind Peanuts:
> - Grind the roasted peanuts into a fine powder using a spice grinder or mortar and pestle.
>
> Mix Suya Spice:
> - In a bowl, combine the ground peanuts with cayenne pepper, paprika, onion powder, garlic powder, ginger powder, ground white pepper, bouillon powder, and salt. Mix well to create the Suya spice mix.

Prepare the Skewers:

> Marinate Meat:
> - Coat the thinly sliced chicken breast or beef with a portion of the Suya spice mix. Ensure that the meat is well coated. Let it marinate for at least 30 minutes to allow the flavors to penetrate.
>
> Skewer the Meat:
> - Thread the marinated meat onto the soaked wooden skewers. Ensure an even distribution of meat on each skewer.
>
> Coat with Spice Mix:
> - Sprinkle additional Suya spice mix over the skewered meat, ensuring an even coating on all sides.

Grill the Suya:

> Preheat Grill or Grill Pan:
> - Preheat an outdoor grill or a grill pan on the stovetop over medium-high heat.
>
> Grill Skewers:
> - Grill the skewers for about 10-15 minutes, turning occasionally to ensure even cooking. The meat should be charred and cooked through.
>
> Check for Doneness:
> - Ensure that the chicken is cooked through, and the beef is cooked to your desired level of doneness.
>
> Serve:
> - Remove the Suya skewers from the grill. Serve them hot with sliced onions, tomatoes, cucumber, and optionally, spicy pepper sauce on the side.
>
> Enjoy:
> - Suya is best enjoyed immediately while hot. The combination of the spicy, peanut-flavored spice mix with the grilled meat and fresh vegetables creates a delicious and satisfying experience.

Suya is a beloved Nigerian street food that showcases the rich and diverse flavors of Nigerian cuisine. The spice mix, with its unique blend of peanuts and aromatic spices, is what sets Suya apart and makes it a flavorful and memorable dish.

Kefta Tagine (Morocco)

Ingredients:

For the Kefta (Meatballs):

- 1 lb ground beef or lamb
- 1 small onion, finely grated
- 2 cloves garlic, minced
- 1/4 cup fresh parsley, finely chopped
- 1 teaspoon ground cumin
- 1 teaspoon ground coriander
- 1 teaspoon paprika
- Salt and black pepper to taste
- 1 egg (optional, for binding)

For the Tomato Sauce:

- 2 tablespoons olive oil
- 1 onion, finely chopped
- 2 cloves garlic, minced
- 1 can (14 oz) diced tomatoes
- 1 tablespoon tomato paste
- 1 teaspoon ground cumin
- 1 teaspoon ground coriander
- 1 teaspoon paprika
- 1/2 teaspoon cinnamon
- Pinch of saffron threads (optional)
- Salt and black pepper to taste
- 1 cup vegetable or beef broth

Additional Ingredients:

- Fresh cilantro or parsley for garnish
- Eggs (optional, for poaching)

Instructions:

Prepare the Kefta:

    Mix Ingredients:

- In a large bowl, combine ground beef or lamb with grated onion, minced garlic, chopped parsley, ground cumin, ground coriander, paprika, salt, and black pepper. Optionally, add an egg to bind the mixture.

Shape Kefta:
- Shape the seasoned meat mixture into small balls or cylindrical shapes. Set aside.

Cook the Tomato Sauce:

Sauté Onion and Garlic:
- In a tagine or a large skillet, heat olive oil over medium heat. Sauté finely chopped onion and minced garlic until softened.

Add Spices:
- Add ground cumin, ground coriander, paprika, cinnamon, and saffron threads (if using). Stir to coat the onions in the spices.

Incorporate Tomato Paste and Diced Tomatoes:
- Add tomato paste and diced tomatoes to the pot. Stir well to combine.

Season and Simmer:
- Season the tomato sauce with salt and black pepper. Pour in the vegetable or beef broth. Let the sauce simmer for about 15-20 minutes, allowing the flavors to meld.

Add Kefta to the Sauce:

Place Kefta in Sauce:
- Gently place the shaped kefta into the simmering tomato sauce. Ensure that the kefta is partially submerged in the sauce.

Simmer Kefta:
- Let the kefta simmer in the sauce for an additional 20-25 minutes, or until the meatballs are cooked through.

Optional: Poach Eggs:

Create Wells:
- If you want to poach eggs in the tagine, create small wells in the tomato sauce and kefta mixture.

Crack Eggs:
- Crack eggs into the wells. Cover the tagine or skillet and let the eggs poach for about 5-7 minutes or until the whites are set but the yolks are still runny.

Garnish and Serve:

Garnish with Fresh Herbs:

- Sprinkle fresh cilantro or parsley over the kefta and tomato sauce.

Serve Hot:
- Kefta Tagine is ready to be served. Serve it hot with crusty bread, couscous, or rice.

Kefta Tagine is a flavorful and comforting dish that reflects the rich culinary tradition of Morocco. The combination of aromatic spices, tomato sauce, and tender meatballs makes it a delightful and satisfying meal. Enjoy the tagine straight from the pot, savoring the unique flavors of Moroccan cuisine.

Papaya Salad (East Africa)

Ingredients:

For the Salad:

- 1 medium-sized ripe papaya, peeled, seeded, and julienned
- 1 cucumber, julienned
- 1 carrot, peeled and julienned
- 1 bell pepper (red, yellow, or green), thinly sliced
- 1 small red onion, thinly sliced
- 1 cup cherry tomatoes, halved
- Fresh cilantro or mint leaves for garnish

For the Dressing:

- 2 tablespoons lime juice
- 1 tablespoon fish sauce (or soy sauce for a vegetarian version)
- 1 tablespoon honey or sugar
- 1 clove garlic, minced
- 1 small red chili, finely chopped (adjust to taste)
- Salt and pepper to taste

Instructions:

Prepare the Salad:

    Prepare Papaya:
- Peel, seed, and julienne the ripe papaya. You can use a julienne peeler or knife for this.

    Prepare Vegetables:
- Julienne the cucumber, carrot, and bell pepper. Thinly slice the red onion. Halve the cherry tomatoes.

    Combine Ingredients:
- In a large bowl, combine the julienned papaya, cucumber, carrot, bell pepper, red onion, and cherry tomatoes. Toss the ingredients gently to mix them evenly.

Prepare the Dressing:

    Mix Lime Juice and Fish Sauce:
- In a small bowl, whisk together lime juice and fish sauce (or soy sauce for a vegetarian version).

    Add Sweetener and Aromatics:

- Add honey or sugar to the lime-fish sauce mixture. Stir in minced garlic and finely chopped red chili. Mix well.

Adjust Seasoning:
- Taste the dressing and adjust the flavor by adding salt and pepper as needed. You can also adjust the sweetness or acidity to your preference.

Assemble the Salad:

Pour Dressing:
- Pour the prepared dressing over the julienned fruits and vegetables.

Toss Gently:
- Toss the salad gently to ensure that the dressing coats all the ingredients.

Chill (Optional):
- If you prefer a chilled salad, refrigerate it for about 30 minutes before serving.

Garnish:
- Garnish the papaya salad with fresh cilantro or mint leaves for added freshness.

Serve:
- Papaya salad is ready to be served. Enjoy it as a light and refreshing side dish or add grilled chicken or shrimp for a complete meal.

Papaya salad is a wonderful way to showcase the vibrant and tropical flavors of East Africa. The combination of ripe papaya with crisp vegetables and a zesty dressing creates a dish that is both colorful and delicious. It's a perfect option for warm days or as a side dish to complement various main courses.

Akara (West Africa)

Ingredients:

- 2 cups black-eyed peas or cowpeas
- 1 medium-sized onion, chopped
- 1-2 fresh chili peppers, chopped (adjust to taste)
- 1 teaspoon ground crayfish (optional)
- Salt to taste
- Vegetable oil for frying

Instructions:

Prepare the Black-Eyed Peas:

Soak the Peas:
- Place the black-eyed peas in a bowl and cover them with water. Allow them to soak for at least 4 hours or overnight.

Remove Skins:
- After soaking, the skins of the black-eyed peas should loosen. Rub the peas between your hands to remove the skins. Rinse the peeled peas thoroughly.

Blend the Peas:
- In a blender or food processor, blend the peeled black-eyed peas with a minimal amount of water until you get a smooth, thick paste. The goal is to achieve a smooth consistency without making the batter too watery.

Prepare the Akara Batter:

Add Seasonings:
- Transfer the blended peas to a bowl. Add the chopped onions, chili peppers, ground crayfish (if using), and salt to taste. Mix the ingredients well.

Whisk or Beat:
- Whisk or beat the mixture vigorously for about 5-10 minutes. This process helps incorporate air into the batter, making the Akara light and fluffy.

Fry the Akara:

Heat Oil:
- In a deep frying pan or pot, heat enough vegetable oil for deep frying. The oil should be hot but not smoking.

Test the Oil:

- To check if the oil is ready, drop a small amount of the Akara batter into the oil. If it sizzles and rises to the top, the oil is hot enough.

Form and Fry:
- Using a spoon or your hands, drop small portions of the Akara batter into the hot oil. Fry until golden brown, turning them occasionally for even cooking.

Drain Excess Oil:
- Once the Akara balls are golden brown and crispy, use a slotted spoon to remove them from the oil. Place them on a plate lined with paper towels to drain excess oil.

Repeat the Process:
- Continue the process until all the Akara batter is used.

Serve:

Enjoy Warm:
- Akara is best enjoyed warm. Serve it as a snack, breakfast item, or alongside a dipping sauce or spicy pepper sauce.

Optional: Serve with Pap:
- In some regions, Akara is commonly served with a side of pap (a porridge made from fermented maize or sorghum) or bread.

Akara is a delightful and versatile dish that can be enjoyed in various ways. Whether served as a snack, breakfast, or part of a larger meal, its crispy exterior and soft, flavorful interior make it a favorite across West Africa.

Chicken Yassa (Senegal)

Ingredients:

For the Marinade:

- 4-6 chicken pieces (drumsticks, thighs, or a whole chicken, cut into pieces)
- 4 large onions, thinly sliced
- 4 cloves garlic, minced
- 2 teaspoons ginger, grated
- 2-3 bay leaves
- 1-2 hot chili peppers, finely chopped (adjust to taste)
- 2 lemons or limes, juiced
- 1/2 cup vegetable oil
- Salt and black pepper to taste

For Cooking:

- 1 cup water
- 2 tablespoons Dijon mustard
- 2 tablespoons white vinegar
- 1 tablespoon sugar (optional, to balance the acidity)
- 1/2 cup green olives (optional, for garnish)
- Fresh parsley or cilantro for garnish

Instructions:

Marinate the Chicken:

    Prepare Marinade:
- In a large bowl, combine sliced onions, minced garlic, grated ginger, bay leaves, chopped chili peppers, lemon or lime juice, vegetable oil, salt, and black pepper. Mix well to create the marinade.

    Marinate Chicken:
- Place the chicken pieces in the marinade, ensuring they are well-coated. Cover the bowl and refrigerate for at least 4 hours or overnight for the flavors to infuse.

Cook the Chicken:

    Preheat Oven or Grill:
- Preheat your oven to 375°F (190°C) or prepare a grill for indirect grilling.

    Transfer to Cooking Dish:

- Transfer the marinated chicken and onions to a baking dish. Spread them out evenly.

Prepare Cooking Liquid:
- In a separate bowl, mix water, Dijon mustard, white vinegar, and sugar (if using). Stir well to combine.

Pour Cooking Liquid:
- Pour the cooking liquid mixture over the chicken and onions in the baking dish.

Cover and Cook:
- Cover the baking dish with aluminum foil or a lid. Place it in the preheated oven or on the grill. Bake for about 45 minutes to 1 hour, or until the chicken is cooked through and tender.

Optional: Grill for Char Flavor (Optional):
- If using a grill, you can finish the chicken by placing it over direct heat for a few minutes on each side to achieve a charred and grilled flavor.

Garnish and Serve:
- Garnish the Chicken Yassa with green olives (if using) and fresh parsley or cilantro.

Serve Warm:
- Chicken Yassa is traditionally served with rice, couscous, or bread. The flavorful onion sauce created during cooking is a key element of the dish.

Chicken Yassa is known for its delicious combination of tangy, spicy, and savory flavors. The marinade and slow cooking process result in tender and flavorful chicken that is enjoyed by many in Senegal and beyond.

Koshari (Sudan)

Ingredients:

For the Koshari:

- 1 cup brown lentils, rinsed
- 1 cup long-grain rice
- 1 cup small pasta (e.g., elbow macaroni or small shells)
- 1 can (14 oz) chickpeas, drained and rinsed
- 1 large onion, thinly sliced
- 3 tablespoons vegetable oil
- Salt to taste

For the Tomato Sauce:

- 1 can (14 oz) crushed tomatoes
- 2 cloves garlic, minced
- 1 teaspoon ground cumin
- 1 teaspoon ground coriander
- 1 teaspoon ground cinnamon
- Salt and black pepper to taste
- 2 tablespoons olive oil

For Garnish:

- Crispy fried onions (store-bought or homemade)
- Chopped fresh parsley or cilantro

Instructions:

Cook the Lentils:

> Boil Lentils:
> - In a pot, combine the rinsed brown lentils with enough water to cover them. Bring to a boil, then reduce heat and simmer until the lentils are tender but not mushy (about 20-25 minutes). Add salt to taste.
>
> Drain Excess Water:
> - Drain any excess water from the lentils and set aside.

Cook the Rice and Pasta:

Cook Rice:
- In a separate pot, cook the rice according to package instructions. Add salt to taste.

Cook Pasta:
- Cook the pasta in a pot of boiling salted water until al dente. Drain and set aside.

Prepare the Tomato Sauce:

Sauté Garlic:
- In a saucepan, heat olive oil over medium heat. Add minced garlic and sauté until fragrant.

Add Crushed Tomatoes:
- Pour in the crushed tomatoes and stir well.

Season the Sauce:
- Add ground cumin, ground coriander, ground cinnamon, salt, and black pepper to the tomato sauce. Stir to combine.

Simmer:
- Allow the sauce to simmer for about 15-20 minutes, stirring occasionally, until it thickens.

Assemble the Koshari:

Layer Ingredients:
- In a large serving dish, layer the cooked lentils, rice, pasta, and chickpeas.

Pour Tomato Sauce:
- Pour the prepared tomato sauce over the layers of lentils, rice, pasta, and chickpeas.

Toss Gently:
- Gently toss the ingredients together to ensure even distribution of the tomato sauce.

Garnish:
- Garnish the Koshari with crispy fried onions and chopped fresh parsley or cilantro.

Serve:
- Koshari is ready to be served. Serve it warm with additional fried onions on the side and your favorite spicy condiments if desired.

Koshari is a delicious and comforting dish that brings together a variety of textures and flavors. The combination of lentils, rice, pasta, and a spiced tomato sauce creates a satisfying and nutritious meal. Enjoy the diverse and flavorful cuisine of Sudan with this hearty Koshari recipe.

Mozambican Prawn Curry (Mozambique)

Ingredients:

- 1 lb large prawns, peeled and deveined
- 2 tablespoons vegetable oil
- 1 onion, finely chopped
- 2 cloves garlic, minced
- 1 tablespoon ginger, grated
- 1 red bell pepper, diced
- 1 yellow bell pepper, diced
- 1 can (14 oz) diced tomatoes
- 1 can (14 oz) coconut milk
- 1 tablespoon tomato paste
- 2 teaspoons ground coriander
- 2 teaspoons ground cumin
- 1 teaspoon turmeric
- 1 teaspoon paprika
- 1 teaspoon chili powder (adjust to taste)
- Salt and black pepper to taste
- Fresh cilantro for garnish
- Cooked rice for serving

Instructions:

Prepare Prawns:
- Peel and devein the prawns, leaving the tails intact.

Sauté Aromatics:
- In a large pan or pot, heat vegetable oil over medium heat. Add finely chopped onion and sauté until it becomes translucent. Add minced garlic and grated ginger, and sauté for an additional 2-3 minutes until fragrant.

Add Bell Peppers:
- Add diced red and yellow bell peppers to the pan. Sauté for a few minutes until the peppers start to soften.

Spice it Up:
- Stir in ground coriander, ground cumin, turmeric, paprika, and chili powder. Mix the spices with the vegetables until well combined.

Tomato Base:

- Add diced tomatoes and tomato paste to the pan. Cook for a few minutes until the tomatoes break down and the mixture becomes slightly thickened.

Coconut Milk Magic:
- Pour in the coconut milk, stirring to combine. Bring the mixture to a gentle simmer.

Season and Simmer:
- Season the curry with salt and black pepper to taste. Allow it to simmer for about 10-15 minutes to let the flavors meld.

Add Prawns:
- Gently add the peeled and deveined prawns to the simmering curry. Cook until the prawns turn pink and are cooked through. Be careful not to overcook them, as prawns can become tough.

Garnish:
- Garnish the Mozambican Prawn Curry with fresh cilantro.

Serve:
- Serve the prawn curry over cooked rice or with your preferred side. Enjoy the rich and flavorful Mozambican dish!

Mozambican Prawn Curry is a delightful and aromatic dish that highlights the delicious seafood of the region. The combination of spices, coconut milk, and fresh prawns creates a memorable culinary experience. Serve it with rice or bread to soak up the flavorful sauce and enjoy the unique flavors of Mozambique.

Plasas (Liberia)

Ingredients:

For the Cassava Leaves:

- 4 cups fresh cassava leaves, washed and finely chopped
- 2 lbs meat (chicken, goat, or beef), cut into bite-sized pieces
- 1 cup smoked fish or dried fish, shredded
- 1 cup palm oil
- 1 large onion, finely chopped
- 2-3 Scotch bonnet peppers, finely chopped (adjust to taste)
- 3 cloves garlic, minced
- 1 tablespoon ground crayfish (optional)
- Salt and black pepper to taste

For the Rice:

- 2 cups rice
- Water for cooking rice

Instructions:

Prepare Cassava Leaves:

Cook Meat:
- In a large pot, cook the meat pieces with salt and black pepper until they are browned and cooked through.

Prepare Palm Oil:
- In a separate pot, heat the palm oil over medium heat. Add chopped onions and minced garlic. Sauté until the onions are translucent.

Add Cassava Leaves:
- Add the finely chopped cassava leaves to the pot with palm oil. Stir well to coat the leaves with the oil.

Combine Meat and Fish:
- Add the cooked meat, shredded smoked or dried fish, and ground crayfish (if using) to the pot. Mix everything together.

Add Pepper and Seasoning:
- Add chopped Scotch bonnet peppers and additional salt and black pepper to taste. Stir to combine.

Simmer:

- Allow the cassava leaves mixture to simmer over medium-low heat for about 1-2 hours, stirring occasionally. This allows the flavors to meld, and the leaves to become tender.

Prepare Rice:

Rinse Rice:
- Rinse the rice thoroughly under cold water until the water runs clear.

Cook Rice:
- In a separate pot, cook the rice according to package instructions. Typically, rice is cooked with water in a ratio of 1:2 (1 cup rice to 2 cups water).

Serve:
- Serve the Plasas over a bed of cooked rice. The combination of the flavorful greens with the rice makes for a hearty and satisfying meal.

Plasas is a nutritious and comforting dish enjoyed in Liberian cuisine. The use of cassava leaves, along with the combination of meat and fish, creates a rich and flavorful stew. It's often served with rice, the staple food in Liberia, making it a complete and delicious meal.

Braaivleis (South Africa)

Ingredients:

For the Meat:

- Various cuts of meat (beef, lamb, pork, chicken, or game meat)
- Marinade or spice rub of your choice (optional)
- Salt and pepper to taste

For the Fire:

- Hardwood or charcoal
- Firelighters or newspaper
- Matches or a fire starter

Instructions:

Prepare the Fire:

Select Wood or Charcoal:
- Choose hardwood, such as hardwood chunks or briquettes, for a traditional braai. Alternatively, charcoal can be used.

Create a Fire Bed:
- Arrange the wood or charcoal in a pile, leaving space for airflow. You can create a pyramid or use a portable braai (barbecue) with a grid.

Light the Fire:
- Use firelighters or crumpled newspaper to ignite the wood or charcoal. Wait until the flames die down, and the coals are covered with white ash.

Adjust Heat:
- Spread the coals for high heat or keep them closer together for lower heat. The temperature of the braai can be adjusted by raising or lowering the grid.

Prepare the Meat:

Select Meat Cuts:
- Choose a variety of meats, such as steaks, chops, boerewors (sausages), lamb ribs, or chicken pieces.

Marinate or Season (Optional):

- Marinate the meat in your favorite South African braai marinade or simply season it with salt and pepper. Popular marinades often include a mix of garlic, herbs, lemon, and spices.

Allow Meat to Reach Room Temperature:
- Take the meat out of the refrigerator and allow it to come to room temperature before placing it on the braai.

Braai the Meat:

Place Meat on the Grid:
- Once the coals are ready, place the meat on the braai grid over the open flame. Allow it to cook evenly on both sides.

Check Doneness:
- Use a meat thermometer or check the meat's doneness by touch. Different cuts and preferences may require various cooking times.

Baste if Desired:
- Baste the meat with additional marinade or sauce during the cooking process if desired.

Rest the Meat:
- Allow the cooked meat to rest for a few minutes before serving. This helps the juices redistribute within the meat.

Serve and Enjoy:

Serve with Accompaniments:
- Braaivleis is often served with side dishes like salads, bread, or South African favorites like boerewors rolls.

Enjoy the Braai:
- Braai is not just about the food; it's a social event. Enjoy the time spent around the fire with family and friends, sharing stories and creating lasting memories.

Braaivleis is a quintessential South African experience that goes beyond the act of cooking meat. It's a cultural tradition, a social gathering, and a celebration of good food and company. The aroma of the open flame and the sizzle of meat on the braai create an atmosphere that is uniquely South African.

Sosatie (South Africa)

Ingredients:

For the Marinade:

- 2 lbs lamb, beef, or chicken, cut into bite-sized cubes
- 1 cup plain yogurt
- 1/4 cup vegetable oil
- 1/4 cup apricot jam
- 2 tablespoons curry powder
- 2 teaspoons ground coriander
- 2 teaspoons ground cumin
- 2 teaspoons ground turmeric
- 2 teaspoons paprika
- 4 cloves garlic, minced
- 2 tablespoons fresh ginger, grated
- Salt and black pepper to taste

For Skewering:

- Wooden or metal skewers (if using wooden skewers, soak them in water for at least 30 minutes to prevent burning)

Instructions:

Prepare the Marinade:

    Combine Ingredients:
- In a bowl, whisk together yogurt, vegetable oil, apricot jam, curry powder, ground coriander, ground cumin, ground turmeric, paprika, minced garlic, grated ginger, salt, and black pepper.

    Marinate the Meat:
- Place the meat cubes in a large dish or resealable plastic bag. Pour the marinade over the meat, ensuring all pieces are well coated. Cover and refrigerate for at least 4 hours or overnight for the flavors to infuse.

Skewer and Grill:

    Preheat the Grill:
- Preheat the grill or braai to medium-high heat.

    Skewer the Meat:

- Thread the marinated meat cubes onto the skewers, alternating with any desired vegetables like bell peppers, onions, or mushrooms.

Baste with Marinade:
- Reserve some of the marinade for basting. Brush the skewered meat with the marinade during grilling.

Grill the Sosaties:
- Place the skewers on the preheated grill and cook, turning occasionally, until the meat is browned and cooked to your desired doneness.

Baste During Cooking:
- Baste the skewers with the reserved marinade during the cooking process to add extra flavor.

Serve Warm:
- Once the meat is cooked through and has a delicious grilled exterior, remove the skewers from the grill.

Garnish (Optional):
- Garnish the Sosaties with fresh herbs like cilantro or parsley if desired.

Serve with Side Dishes:
- Sosaties are often served with side dishes like rice, couscous, or bread. They can also be enjoyed on their own as a flavorful appetizer or main dish.

Sosaties are a popular choice for South African gatherings and braais. The combination of the sweet and savory marinade with the grilled meat creates a delicious and aromatic dish that captures the essence of South African cuisine. Enjoy these skewers with friends and family, celebrating the vibrant flavors of the rainbow nation.

Kedjenou (Ivory Coast)

Ingredients:

- 1 whole chicken or guinea fowl, cut into pieces
- 2 large onions, finely chopped
- 2-3 tomatoes, chopped
- 2 bell peppers (red and green), sliced
- 2 eggplants, sliced
- 4-6 okra pods, sliced (optional)
- 4 cloves garlic, minced
- 2 tablespoons ginger, grated
- 2-3 hot chili peppers, chopped (adjust to taste)
- 2 bay leaves
- 1 teaspoon thyme
- 1 teaspoon curry powder
- 1 teaspoon paprika
- 1/2 cup vegetable oil
- Salt and black pepper to taste
- Banana leaves or parchment paper for sealing the pot

Instructions:

Prepare Chicken or Guinea Fowl:
- Clean and cut the chicken or guinea fowl into serving pieces. Rub the pieces with salt, black pepper, and a bit of grated ginger.

Marinate:
- In a large bowl, combine the chicken or guinea fowl pieces with minced garlic, grated ginger, curry powder, paprika, thyme, salt, and black pepper. Let it marinate for at least 30 minutes to allow the flavors to penetrate.

Sauté Vegetables:
- In a large pot or Dutch oven, heat vegetable oil over medium heat. Add finely chopped onions and sauté until translucent.

Add Tomatoes and Peppers:
- Add chopped tomatoes and sliced bell peppers to the pot. Cook until the vegetables soften.

Layer the Pot:
- Layer the marinated chicken or guinea fowl pieces on top of the sautéed vegetables.

Add Remaining Vegetables:

- Place sliced eggplants, okra (if using), chopped hot chili peppers, bay leaves, and additional thyme on top of the meat.

Seal the Pot:
- Cover the pot tightly with banana leaves or parchment paper. Seal the edges with a lid or foil to trap the steam during cooking.

Cook Slowly:
- Place the sealed pot in an oven preheated to around 350°F (180°C) or on the stovetop over low heat. Let it cook slowly for 1.5 to 2 hours. The slow cooking allows the flavors to meld, and the meat becomes tender.

Check Doneness:
- Check for doneness by ensuring the meat is fully cooked and tender. The vegetables should be soft and infused with the flavors.

Serve:
- Kedjenou is traditionally served with rice or a starchy side like yams or plantains.

Kedjenou is a hearty and flavorful dish that showcases the rich culinary heritage of Ivory Coast. The slow-cooking method allows the ingredients to meld into a delicious and aromatic stew. The sealing technique with banana leaves or parchment paper is a distinctive feature of this traditional dish. Enjoy the communal and savory experience of Kedjenou with family and friends.

Dolma (North Africa)

Ingredients:

For the Grape Leaves:

- Grape leaves (fresh or preserved, available in jars)
- Water for soaking (if using preserved grape leaves)

For the Filling:

- 1 cup rice (medium or short-grain)
- 1 cup water
- 1/2 cup pine nuts, toasted
- 1/2 cup currants or raisins
- 1/4 cup fresh mint, chopped
- 1/4 cup fresh dill, chopped
- 1/4 cup fresh parsley, chopped
- 1 onion, finely chopped
- 2 cloves garlic, minced
- 1/4 cup olive oil
- Juice of 1 lemon
- Salt and pepper to taste

For Cooking:

- Lemon slices
- Olive oil
- Water

Instructions:

Prepare the Grape Leaves:

> If Using Fresh Grape Leaves:
> - Blanch the fresh grape leaves in boiling water for 1-2 minutes. Drain and set aside.
>
> If Using Preserved Grape Leaves:
> - If the grape leaves are preserved in brine, rinse them under cold water to remove excess salt. Soak them in warm water for about 10-15 minutes to soften. Drain and set aside.

Prepare the Filling:

Cook Rice:
- In a saucepan, combine the rice and water. Bring to a boil, then reduce heat, cover, and simmer until the rice is cooked and the water is absorbed.

Toast Pine Nuts:
- In a dry skillet, toast the pine nuts over medium heat until they are golden brown. Be careful not to burn them.

Prepare Filling:
- In a bowl, combine the cooked rice, toasted pine nuts, currants or raisins, chopped mint, dill, parsley, chopped onion, minced garlic, olive oil, lemon juice, salt, and pepper. Mix well.

Assemble and Cook:

Fill Grape Leaves:
- Lay a grape leaf flat on a work surface, shiny side down. Place a small amount of the rice mixture in the center of the leaf.

Fold and Roll:
- Fold the sides of the grape leaf over the filling, then roll it tightly from the bottom to the top, forming a compact roll.

Repeat:
- Repeat the process until all the grape leaves are filled and rolled.

Layer in a Pot:
- In a wide and deep pot, arrange the Dolma rolls in layers, placing lemon slices between the layers.

Cook:
- Drizzle olive oil over the top layer of Dolma. Add enough water to the pot to almost cover the Dolma. Place a heavy plate or lid on top to keep the Dolma in place during cooking.

Simmer:
- Simmer the Dolma over low heat for about 45 minutes to 1 hour, or until the rice is fully cooked and the grape leaves are tender.

Serve:
- Once cooked, let the Dolma cool slightly before serving. Serve with yogurt or a dipping sauce of your choice.

Dolma is a delightful and versatile dish, and variations of it are found in many regions. This recipe offers a vegetarian version, but you can also include minced meat in the filling if desired. The combination of grape leaves, flavorful rice, and aromatic herbs creates a delicious and satisfying dish.

Kitcha Fit-Fit (Eritrea)

Ingredients:

- Injera (store-bought or homemade)
- 2 tablespoons Niter Kibbeh (seasoned clarified butter) or olive oil
- 1 onion, finely chopped
- 2 tomatoes, chopped
- 1 green chili pepper, finely chopped (adjust to taste)
- 1 teaspoon berbere spice (adjust to taste)
- Salt to taste
- Fresh cilantro or parsley, chopped (for garnish)

Instructions:

Prepare Injera:
- If you are using store-bought injera, you can use it as is. If making it at home, ensure that the injera is slightly aged or dry.

Tear Injera:
- Tear the injera into bite-sized pieces. You can tear it into small or larger pieces, depending on your preference.

Sauté Onion and Chili:
- In a pan, heat Niter Kibbeh or olive oil over medium heat. Add finely chopped onion and green chili pepper. Sauté until the onion becomes translucent.

Add Tomatoes and Berbere:
- Add chopped tomatoes to the pan and cook until they soften. Stir in berbere spice and mix well with the tomatoes and onions. Adjust the spice level according to your taste.

Toss Injera:
- Add the torn injera pieces to the pan. Toss the injera in the seasoned mixture, ensuring that the injera pieces are well-coated.

Season and Mix:
- Season the Kitcha Fit-Fit with salt to taste. Mix everything well, ensuring that the injera absorbs the flavors of the seasoned mixture.

Garnish:
- Garnish the Kitcha Fit-Fit with chopped fresh cilantro or parsley for added freshness.

Serve Warm:

- Kitcha Fit-Fit is traditionally served warm. It can be enjoyed on its own or served with yogurt on the side.

Kitcha Fit-Fit is a simple yet flavorful dish that highlights the unique taste and texture of injera. The combination of spices, tomatoes, and injera creates a dish that is both satisfying and comforting. It is a popular choice for breakfast or a light meal in Eritrea, and it provides a delicious way to use leftover injera.

Yassa Poulet (Senegal)

Ingredients:

For the Marinade:

- 4-6 chicken pieces (drumsticks, thighs, or a whole chicken, cut into pieces)
- 4 large onions, thinly sliced
- 4 cloves garlic, minced
- 2 teaspoons ginger, grated
- 2-3 bay leaves
- 2-3 lemons, juiced
- 1/2 cup vegetable oil
- 1 tablespoon Dijon mustard
- 1 teaspoon red pepper flakes (adjust to taste)
- Salt and black pepper to taste

For Cooking:

- 1 cup water
- 2-3 tablespoons vegetable oil
- 1/2 cup green olives (optional, for garnish)
- Fresh parsley or cilantro for garnish

Instructions:

Marinate the Chicken:

Prepare Marinade:
- In a large bowl, combine sliced onions, minced garlic, grated ginger, bay leaves, lemon juice, vegetable oil, Dijon mustard, red pepper flakes, salt, and black pepper. Mix well to create the marinade.

Marinate Chicken:
- Place the chicken pieces in the marinade, ensuring they are well-coated. Cover the bowl and refrigerate for at least 4 hours or overnight for the flavors to infuse.

Cook the Chicken:

Preheat Oven or Grill:
- Preheat your oven to 375°F (190°C) or prepare a grill for indirect grilling.

Transfer to Cooking Dish:
- Transfer the marinated chicken and onions to a baking dish. Spread them out evenly.

Prepare Cooking Liquid:
- In a bowl, mix water and additional vegetable oil. Pour the mixture over the chicken and onions in the baking dish.

Cover and Cook:
- Cover the baking dish with aluminum foil or a lid. Place it in the preheated oven or on the grill. Bake for about 45 minutes to 1 hour, or until the chicken is cooked through and tender.

Optional: Grill for Char Flavor (Optional):
- If using a grill, you can finish the chicken by placing it over direct heat for a few minutes on each side to achieve a charred and grilled flavor.

Garnish and Serve:
- Garnish Yassa Poulet with green olives (if using) and fresh parsley or cilantro.

Serve Warm:
- Yassa Poulet is traditionally served with rice or couscous, and the flavorful onion sauce created during cooking is a key element of the dish.

Yassa Poulet is a delightful and savory dish that showcases the vibrant flavors of Senegalese cuisine. The combination of tangy marinade

Tajine el Khodar (Algeria)

Ingredients:

- 2 tablespoons olive oil
- 1 onion, finely chopped
- 2 cloves garlic, minced
- 1 teaspoon ground cumin
- 1 teaspoon ground coriander
- 1 teaspoon ground turmeric
- 1 teaspoon paprika
- 1 teaspoon ground cinnamon
- 1/2 teaspoon ground ginger
- 1/2 teaspoon cayenne pepper (adjust to taste)
- Salt and black pepper to taste
- 1 cup chickpeas, cooked (canned or pre-cooked)
- 2 carrots, peeled and sliced
- 1 sweet potato, peeled and diced
- 1 zucchini, sliced
- 1 eggplant, diced
- 1 bell pepper, sliced
- 1 cup cherry tomatoes, halved
- 1 cup vegetable broth or water
- Fresh parsley or cilantro for garnish
- Lemon wedges for serving
- Cooked couscous or rice for serving

Instructions:

Sauté Aromatics:
- In a large tagine or a heavy-bottomed pot, heat olive oil over medium heat. Add finely chopped onion and minced garlic. Sauté until the onions are soft and translucent.

Add Spices:
- Add ground cumin, ground coriander, ground turmeric, paprika, ground cinnamon, ground ginger, cayenne pepper, salt, and black pepper to the sautéed onions. Stir well to coat the onions in the spices.

Add Vegetables:

- Add the chickpeas, sliced carrots, diced sweet potato, sliced zucchini, diced eggplant, sliced bell pepper, and halved cherry tomatoes to the tagine. Mix the vegetables with the spices.

Pour Broth:
- Pour vegetable broth or water over the vegetable mixture. Stir to combine.

Simmer:
- Cover the tagine or pot and let the mixture simmer over medium-low heat for about 30-40 minutes or until the vegetables are tender. Stir occasionally to ensure even cooking.

Check Seasoning:
- Taste and adjust the seasoning if needed. Add more salt, pepper, or spices according to your preference.

Garnish and Serve:
- Garnish Tajine el Khodar with fresh parsley or cilantro. Serve it over cooked couscous or rice.

Serve with Lemon Wedges:
- Serve Tajine el Khodar with lemon wedges on the side. Squeezing fresh lemon juice over the dish adds a bright and citrusy flavor.

Tajine el Khodar is a delightful and comforting Algerian dish that celebrates the rich flavors of vegetables and aromatic spices. It's a versatile dish that can be enjoyed on its own or paired with couscous or rice. The slow simmering process allows the vegetables to absorb the spices, creating a delicious and fragrant tagine. Enjoy this flavorful Algerian culinary experience!

Efo Elegusi (Nigeria)

Ingredients:

For the Egusi Paste:

- 1 cup ground egusi (melon seeds)
- 1/4 cup water (for blending)
- 1 small onion, chopped

For the Soup:

- 2 cups assorted meats (beef, goat meat, tripe, or cow's skin), cut into bite-sized pieces
- 1 cup smoked fish or stockfish, deboned and flaked
- 1 cup chopped spinach or other leafy greens (ugu, waterleaf, or amaranth leaves)
- 1/2 cup palm oil
- 2 tablespoons ground crayfish
- 2-3 scotch bonnet peppers, blended (adjust to taste)
- 1 large onion, chopped
- 3-4 cups meat or vegetable broth
- Salt and seasoning cubes to taste

Instructions:

Prepare the Egusi Paste:

Blend Egusi:
- In a blender, combine the ground egusi, chopped onion, and water. Blend until you get a smooth paste.

Cook the Meats:

Cook Assorted Meats:
- In a large pot, cook the assorted meats with salt, seasoning cubes, and enough water until they are tender. This may take about 30-40 minutes, depending on the toughness of the meats.

Add Smoked Fish or Stockfish:
- Add the smoked fish or stockfish to the pot and continue cooking for an additional 10-15 minutes.

Set Aside Meat Broth:
- Once the meats are cooked, set aside the broth to be used later.

Prepare the Soup:

Heat Palm Oil:
- In another pot, heat palm oil over medium heat. Allow it to melt but not bleach.

Sauté Onions and Peppers:
- Add chopped onions to the palm oil and sauté until they become translucent. Add blended scotch bonnet peppers and cook for a few more minutes.

Add Egusi Paste:
- Stir in the egusi paste and cook, stirring continuously to prevent lumps, for about 5-8 minutes until the egusi is well-fried and the oil begins to separate.

Add Meat Broth:
- Gradually add the meat or vegetable broth to the pot, stirring continuously to achieve a smooth consistency. Adjust the thickness of the soup by adding more or less broth.

Season and Simmer:
- Add ground crayfish, salt, and seasoning cubes to taste. Allow the soup to simmer for about 10-15 minutes.

Add Cooked Meats:
- Add the cooked assorted meats, smoked fish, and any additional stockfish to the pot. Allow the soup to simmer for an additional 10-15 minutes, allowing the flavors to meld.

Add Leafy Greens:
- Finally, add the chopped spinach or other leafy greens to the pot. Stir well and cook for an additional 5 minutes until the greens are wilted.

Adjust Seasoning:
- Taste and adjust the seasoning if needed. Add more salt or seasoning cubes according to your preference.

Serve:
- Efo Elegusi is traditionally served with a starchy side such as pounded yam, fufu, or rice.

Efo Elegusi is a flavorful and nutritious Nigerian soup that showcases the richness of melon seeds and a variety of meats and fish. Enjoy it as a wholesome and satisfying meal, served alongside your favorite Nigerian staples.

Fried Tilapia (Ghana)

Ingredients:

- 2 whole tilapia fish, cleaned and scaled
- 1 cup all-purpose flour
- 1 teaspoon garlic powder
- 1 teaspoon onion powder
- 1 teaspoon paprika
- 1 teaspoon cayenne pepper (adjust to taste)
- Salt and black pepper to taste
- Vegetable oil for frying
- Lemon wedges for serving

Instructions:

Clean and Scale Tilapia:
- Rinse the tilapia thoroughly and pat them dry with paper towels. Ensure that the scales are removed, and the fish is cleaned inside and out.

Prepare Marinade:
- In a bowl, mix the flour with garlic powder, onion powder, paprika, cayenne pepper, salt, and black pepper. This will be the dry coating for the fish.

Coat Tilapia:
- Lightly coat each tilapia fish with the seasoned flour mixture, ensuring an even coating on both sides. Press the flour mixture onto the fish to adhere.

Heat Vegetable Oil:
- In a large frying pan or deep fryer, heat enough vegetable oil for deep-frying. The oil should be hot but not smoking.

Fry Tilapia:
- Carefully place the coated tilapia in the hot oil, one at a time. Fry until each side is golden brown and the fish is cooked through. This typically takes about 8-10 minutes per side, depending on the size of the fish.

Drain Excess Oil:
- Once fried, use a slotted spoon to carefully remove the tilapia from the oil. Allow the excess oil to drain on paper towels.

Serve:
- Serve the Fried Tilapia hot, garnished with lemon wedges on the side.

Enjoy:
- Fried Tilapia is often enjoyed on its own or served with a side of fried plantains, rice, or a fresh salad.

Tips:

- Make sure the fish is well-coated with the seasoned flour mixture for a crispy exterior.
- Adjust the level of cayenne pepper to your spice preference.
- Use a deep fryer or a large, deep frying pan for even cooking.

Fried Tilapia is a popular and delicious dish in Ghana, loved for its crispy texture and flavorful coating. It's a versatile dish that can be enjoyed on various occasions, whether as a casual meal or part of a festive spread. Serve it with your favorite side dishes and enjoy the rich flavors of Ghanaian cuisine.

Kahawa (East Africa)

Ingredients:

- Coarsely ground East African coffee beans (Arabica beans are commonly used)
- Water
- Sugar (optional)
- Cardamom pods (optional)

Instructions:

Measure Coffee:
- Measure the desired amount of coarsely ground coffee beans. The ratio of coffee to water can be adjusted based on personal preference.

Boil Water:
- Bring water to a boil. The amount of water depends on how many cups of coffee you want to make.

Add Coffee to Boiling Water:
- Once the water is boiling, add the coarsely ground coffee to it. Stir the coffee into the boiling water.

Simmer:
- Allow the coffee to simmer over low to medium heat for about 5-10 minutes. The simmering allows the coffee to steep and extract its flavors.

Add Sugar and Cardamom (Optional):
- If desired, add sugar to sweeten the coffee. Some people also add cardamom pods for additional flavor. Adjust the sweetness and flavorings to your liking.

Strain the Coffee:
- After simmering, strain the coffee to remove the grounds. You can use a fine mesh strainer, cheesecloth, or a traditional East African coffee pot with a built-in filter.

Serve Hot:
- Pour the strained coffee into cups and serve it hot.

Enjoy:
- Enjoy your cup of Kahawa, savoring the rich flavors and aroma. Kahawa is often sipped slowly, providing a moment to relax and socialize.

Additional Tips:

- East African coffee is often enjoyed without milk, but you can add milk if you prefer.
- Experiment with different ratios of coffee to water to find the strength that suits your taste.
- Some variations include adding spices like cinnamon or cloves for extra flavor.

Kahawa is not just a beverage in East Africa; it is a social and cultural experience. It is often prepared and shared during social gatherings, family meetings, or simply as a way to connect with others. The process of making and enjoying Kahawa reflects the region's rich coffee culture and the importance of communal moments around a cup of freshly brewed coffee.

Sorpotel (Goa, influenced by African cuisine)

Ingredients:

For the Sorpotel Paste:

- 10-12 dry red chilies, soaked in warm water
- 1 tablespoon cumin seeds
- 1 tablespoon coriander seeds
- 1 teaspoon black peppercorns
- 1/2 teaspoon mustard seeds
- 1/2 teaspoon turmeric powder
- 8-10 cloves garlic
- 1-inch piece ginger, peeled

For the Sorpotel:

- 1 kg pork meat, diced into small pieces
- 200 grams pork liver, diced
- 2 large onions, finely chopped
- 4-5 green chilies, chopped (adjust to taste)
- 1 cup vinegar
- 1 cup tamarind pulp (soak tamarind in warm water and extract pulp)
- 4-5 bay leaves
- 4-5 cloves
- 2-inch cinnamon stick
- Salt to taste
- Oil for cooking

Instructions:

Prepare Sorpotel Paste:

Grind Spices:

- In a blender, grind soaked red chilies, cumin seeds, coriander seeds, black peppercorns, mustard seeds, turmeric powder, garlic, and ginger into a smooth paste. Add a little water if needed.

Prepare Sorpotel:

Marinate Pork:

- Marinate the diced pork meat and liver with the prepared Sorpotel paste. Ensure the meat is well-coated and let it marinate for at least 2 hours or overnight in the refrigerator.

Cook Marinated Meat:
- In a large pot or pan, heat oil over medium heat. Add chopped onions and green chilies. Sauté until the onions are golden brown.

Add Marinated Meat:
- Add the marinated pork meat and liver to the pot. Cook on medium-high heat until the meat is browned.

Add Vinegar and Tamarind:
- Pour in the vinegar and tamarind pulp. Stir well to combine.

Add Spices:
- Add bay leaves, cloves, and the cinnamon stick to the pot. Season with salt to taste.

Simmer:
- Lower the heat, cover the pot, and let the Sorpotel simmer on low heat for at least 2-3 hours. Stir occasionally to prevent sticking and ensure even cooking.

Check for Doneness:
- Check for doneness by ensuring that the meat is tender and the flavors have melded together.

Adjust Seasoning:
- Adjust the seasoning if needed, adding more salt or tamarind for balance.

Serve:
- Once the Sorpotel is cooked to perfection, remove it from heat. Serve hot with steamed rice or traditional Goan bread.

Sorpotel is a complex and flavorful dish that reflects the cultural influences of Goa's history. The African and Portuguese influences are evident in the use of spices and the cooking techniques. This dish is a celebration of flavors and is often enjoyed during festive occasions, bringing people together to savor the rich and aromatic stew.

Ogbono Soup (Nigeria)

Ingredients:

- 1 cup ground ogbono seeds
- 2 cups assorted meats (beef, goat meat, tripe, or cow's skin), cut into bite-sized pieces
- 1 cup spinach or other leafy greens, chopped
- 1/2 cup palm oil
- 1 large onion, chopped
- 2-3 scotch bonnet peppers, blended (adjust to taste)
- 3-4 cups meat or vegetable broth
- 1 tablespoon ground crayfish
- Salt and seasoning cubes to taste

Instructions:

Prepare Ogbono Paste:
- In a dry pan, toast the ground ogbono seeds over low to medium heat for a few minutes. This helps enhance the flavor. Be careful not to burn them.
- Add the toasted ogbono seeds to a blender or food processor. Add a small amount of water and blend until you get a smooth, thick paste. Set aside.

Cook Assorted Meats:
- In a large pot, cook the assorted meats with salt, seasoning cubes, and enough water until they are tender. This may take about 30-40 minutes, depending on the toughness of the meats.

Set Aside Meat Broth:
- Once the meats are cooked, set aside the broth to be used later.

Heat Palm Oil:
- In another pot, heat palm oil over medium heat. Allow it to melt but not bleach.

Sauté Onions and Peppers:
- Add chopped onions to the palm oil and sauté until they become translucent. Add blended scotch bonnet peppers and cook for a few more minutes.

Add Ogbono Paste:
- Stir in the ogbono paste to the pot. Cook, stirring continuously, for about 5-8 minutes until the ogbono is well-fried and the oil begins to separate.

Add Meat Broth:

- Gradually add the meat or vegetable broth to the pot, stirring continuously to achieve a smooth consistency. Adjust the thickness of the soup by adding more or less broth.

Simmer:
- Allow the soup to simmer over medium-low heat for about 10-15 minutes, stirring occasionally.

Add Cooked Meats:
- Add the cooked assorted meats to the pot. Stir well and let it simmer for an additional 10 minutes.

Season and Add Greens:
- Add ground crayfish, salt, and seasoning cubes to taste. Add the chopped spinach or other leafy greens to the pot. Stir well and let it simmer for another 5 minutes until the greens are wilted.

Adjust Seasoning:
- Taste and adjust the seasoning if needed. Add more salt or seasoning cubes according to your preference.

Serve:
- Ogbono Soup is traditionally served with a starchy side such as fufu, pounded yam, or eba.

Ogbono Soup is a hearty and satisfying Nigerian dish that is cherished for its unique texture and rich flavor. It's a favorite in many households and is often enjoyed as a comfort food. Serve it with your preferred side dish and enjoy the deliciousness of this traditional Nigerian soup.

Chakalaka (South Africa)

Ingredients:

- 2 tablespoons vegetable oil
- 1 large onion, finely chopped
- 2 garlic cloves, minced
- 1 green bell pepper, diced
- 1 red bell pepper, diced
- 2 carrots, grated
- 2 tomatoes, chopped
- 1 can (400g) baked beans in tomato sauce
- 1 teaspoon curry powder
- 1 teaspoon ground paprika
- 1 teaspoon ground cumin
- 1/2 teaspoon chili flakes (adjust to taste)
- Salt and black pepper to taste
- Fresh cilantro or parsley for garnish (optional)

Instructions:

Heat Oil:
- In a large pan, heat the vegetable oil over medium heat.

Sauté Onions and Garlic:
- Add the finely chopped onions and minced garlic to the pan. Sauté until the onions are soft and translucent.

Add Bell Peppers and Carrots:
- Add the diced green and red bell peppers along with the grated carrots to the pan. Stir and cook for a few minutes until the vegetables begin to soften.

Add Tomatoes:
- Add the chopped tomatoes to the pan. Cook until the tomatoes break down and release their juices.

Season with Spices:
- Stir in the curry powder, ground paprika, ground cumin, and chili flakes. Mix well to coat the vegetables with the spices.

Add Baked Beans:
- Pour in the can of baked beans in tomato sauce. Stir to combine with the vegetables and spices.

Simmer:

- Reduce the heat to low and let the Chakalaka simmer for about 15-20 minutes, allowing the flavors to meld. Stir occasionally.

Adjust Seasoning:
- Taste the Chakalaka and adjust the seasoning with salt and black pepper. Add more chili flakes if you prefer a spicier relish.

Garnish and Serve:
- Garnish the Chakalaka with fresh cilantro or parsley if desired. Serve it as a side dish with grilled meats, bread, or rice.

Chakalaka is a colorful and spicy relish that adds a burst of flavor to any meal. It has become a staple in South African cuisine and is often enjoyed as part of a traditional braai. The combination of vegetables and spices creates a delicious and vibrant dish that can be adapted to suit personal preferences.

Moin Moin (Nigeria)

Ingredients:

- 2 cups peeled and washed black-eyed peas
- 1 medium onion, chopped
- 2-3 red bell peppers, chopped
- 2-3 scotch bonnet peppers (adjust to taste)
- 2 cloves garlic
- 1/2 cup vegetable oil
- 1 cup broth or water
- 2 teaspoons ground crayfish (optional)
- 1 teaspoon ground nutmeg or ground cumin
- Salt and pepper to taste
- Banana leaves or foil (for wrapping)
- Optional toppings: sliced boiled eggs, sardines, or cooked vegetables

Instructions:

Prepare the Black-Eyed Peas:
- Soak the black-eyed peas in water for about 1-2 hours to soften them. Drain the water.

Blend the Peas Mixture:
- In a blender, combine the soaked black-eyed peas, chopped onions, red bell peppers, scotch bonnet peppers, and garlic. Blend until you get a smooth batter. Add some water if needed to aid blending.

Cook the Moin Moin Base:
- Pour the blended mixture into a large bowl. Add vegetable oil, broth or water, ground crayfish (if using), ground nutmeg or cumin, salt, and pepper. Mix well.

Prepare Banana Leaves or Foil:
- If using banana leaves, cut them into rectangles and pass them quickly over an open flame to make them pliable. If using foil, cut it into rectangles.

Wrap the Moin Moin:
- Scoop a portion of the Moin Moin mixture onto each piece of banana leaf or foil. You can add optional toppings like sliced boiled eggs, sardines, or cooked vegetables at this point. Fold the banana leaves or foil to form parcels, sealing the edges.

Steam the Moin Moin:

- Place the wrapped Moin Moin parcels in a steamer or in a pot with a steaming rack. Steam for about 45 minutes to 1 hour or until the Moin Moin is set and cooked through.

Serve:
- Once cooked, carefully open the parcels and serve the Moin Moin warm. It can be enjoyed on its own or as a side dish.

Note: You can also bake Moin Moin in the oven by placing the wrapped parcels in a preheated oven at 350°F (180°C) for about 45 minutes to 1 hour.

Moin Moin is a delicious and nutritious dish that is versatile and can be customized to suit personal preferences. It's a popular dish in Nigerian cuisine and is enjoyed by many as a healthy and satisfying meal.

Kunu (Nigeria)

Ingredients:

- 2 cups sorghum or millet
- Water for soaking
- 1 tablespoon ginger, grated
- 1 tablespoon cloves or 2 tablespoons powdered cloves
- Sugar or honey to taste
- Pineapple or orange slices for garnish (optional)

Instructions:

Soak the Grains:
- Rinse the sorghum or millet thoroughly and soak it in water for at least 24 hours. Change the water a couple of times during soaking.

Grind the Grains:
- After soaking, drain the water and grind the soaked sorghum or millet into a smooth paste. You can use a blender or a grinding stone for this purpose.

Extract the Liquid:
- Place the ground sorghum or millet paste in a clean cloth and squeeze to extract the liquid. Collect the liquid in a bowl, and this liquid is known as "kunun."

Fermentation:
- Allow the kunun to ferment for about 48 hours. This fermentation process gives Kunu its distinct taste and a mildly alcoholic content.

Strain the Fermented Liquid:
- After fermentation, strain the liquid to remove any sediment or solid particles. You can use a fine mesh sieve or cheesecloth for this purpose.

Flavoring:
- Add grated ginger and cloves to the strained kunun. Stir well to incorporate the flavors.

Sweeten to Taste:
- Sweeten the Kunu with sugar or honey to your taste preference. Stir until the sweetener is well dissolved.

Serve Chilled:
- Chill the Kunu in the refrigerator for a few hours before serving.

Garnish (Optional):
- Garnish the Kunu with slices of pineapple or orange if desired.

Serve:
- Serve Kunu Zaki chilled in glasses. It can be enjoyed on its own or paired with a snack.

Note: Kunu Zaki is mildly alcoholic due to the fermentation process. If you prefer a non-alcoholic version, you can reduce the fermentation time.

Kunu is not only refreshing but also a good source of nutrients. It is a beverage that is deeply rooted in Nigerian culture and is often prepared for special occasions, celebrations, or simply as a refreshing drink to beat the heat.

Okro Soup (West Africa)

Ingredients:

- 2 cups fresh okra, finely chopped or sliced
- 1 pound assorted meats (beef, goat meat, tripe, or cow's skin), cut into bite-sized pieces
- 1 cup shrimp, peeled and deveined (optional)
- 1/2 cup palm oil
- 1 large onion, finely chopped
- 2-3 scotch bonnet peppers, blended (adjust to taste)
- 3-4 cups meat or vegetable broth
- 1 cup chopped spinach or other leafy greens
- 2 tomatoes, chopped
- 2 tablespoons ground crayfish
- Salt and seasoning cubes to taste

Instructions:

Prepare Okra:
- Wash and finely chop or slice the fresh okra. Set it aside.

Cook Assorted Meats:
- In a large pot, cook the assorted meats with salt, seasoning cubes, and enough water until they are tender. This may take about 30-40 minutes, depending on the toughness of the meats.

Set Aside Meat Broth:
- Once the meats are cooked, set aside the broth to be used later.

Heat Palm Oil:
- In another pot, heat palm oil over medium heat. Allow it to melt but not bleach.

Sauté Onions and Peppers:
- Add chopped onions to the palm oil and sauté until they become translucent. Add blended scotch bonnet peppers and cook for a few more minutes.

Add Tomatoes and Broth:
- Stir in the chopped tomatoes to the pot. Cook until the tomatoes break down and release their juices. Gradually add the meat or vegetable broth to the pot, stirring continuously.

Add Chopped Okra:

- Add the chopped okra to the pot. Stir well to combine with the broth and other ingredients.

Simmer:
- Allow the soup to simmer over medium heat for about 10-15 minutes, stirring occasionally. This helps the okra to release its mucilage and thicken the soup.

Add Cooked Meats and Shrimp:
- Add the cooked assorted meats and peeled shrimp (if using) to the pot. Let it simmer for an additional 10 minutes.

Season and Add Greens:
- Add ground crayfish, salt, and seasoning cubes to taste. Stir in the chopped spinach or other leafy greens. Let it simmer for another 5 minutes until the greens are wilted.

Adjust Seasoning:
- Taste and adjust the seasoning if needed. Add more salt or seasoning cubes according to your preference.

Serve:
- Okro Soup is traditionally served with a starchy side such as fufu, pounded yam, or rice.

Okro Soup is a nutritious and flavorful dish that showcases the versatility of okra. It's a beloved West African recipe that is enjoyed by many for its unique texture and taste. Customize the protein options and adjust the spice level to suit your preferences.

Pulao (North Africa)

Ingredients:

- 1 1/2 cups basmati rice (or any long-grain rice)
- 2 tablespoons vegetable oil or clarified butter (ghee)
- 1 large onion, finely chopped
- 2-3 cloves garlic, minced
- 1 teaspoon ground cumin
- 1 teaspoon ground coriander
- 1/2 teaspoon ground cinnamon
- 1/2 teaspoon ground turmeric
- 1/2 teaspoon paprika
- 1/4 teaspoon cayenne pepper (optional, for heat)
- 2 cups mixed vegetables (carrots, peas, bell peppers, etc.), diced
- 1/4 cup raisins or dried apricots (optional, for sweetness)
- 3 cups chicken or vegetable broth
- Salt to taste
- Chopped fresh cilantro or parsley for garnish

Instructions:

Rinse and Soak Rice:
- Rinse the basmati rice under cold water until the water runs clear. Soak the rice in water for about 30 minutes, then drain.

Sauté Onions and Aromatics:
- In a large pot or Dutch oven, heat the vegetable oil or ghee over medium heat. Add the chopped onions and sauté until they become soft and translucent.

Add Spices:
- Add the minced garlic, ground cumin, ground coriander, ground cinnamon, ground turmeric, paprika, and cayenne pepper (if using). Stir well and sauté for a minute until the spices become fragrant.

Add Vegetables and Raisins:
- Add the mixed vegetables and raisins or dried apricots (if using). Sauté for a few minutes until the vegetables begin to soften.

Add Rice and Toast:
- Add the soaked and drained rice to the pot. Stir well to coat the rice with the spices and vegetables. Allow the rice to toast for a couple of minutes.

Pour in Broth:

- Pour in the chicken or vegetable broth. Season with salt to taste. Bring the mixture to a boil.

Simmer:
- Once boiling, reduce the heat to low, cover the pot with a tight-fitting lid, and let it simmer for about 15-20 minutes or until the rice is cooked and the liquid is absorbed.

Fluff and Garnish:
- Once the rice is cooked, fluff it gently with a fork. Garnish the pulao with chopped fresh cilantro or parsley.

Serve:
- Serve the North African-style pulao as a flavorful side dish or as a main course. It pairs well with grilled meats, fish, or can be enjoyed on its own.

Note:

- You can customize this pulao recipe by adding cooked chicken, lamb, or beef for a protein boost.
- Adjust the spice levels according to your preference.

This North African-style pulao is a fragrant and delicious dish that incorporates the aromatic flavors of the region. It's a versatile dish that can be adapted to suit your taste preferences and is perfect for serving on various occasions.

Bissap Juice (Senegal)

Ingredients:

- 1 cup dried hibiscus petals (bissap)
- 4 cups water
- 1 cup pineapple juice
- 1/2 cup orange juice
- 1/2 cup sugar (adjust to taste)
- Fresh mint leaves for garnish (optional)
- Ice cubes (optional)

Instructions:

Rinse and Soak Hibiscus Petals:
- Rinse the dried hibiscus petals thoroughly under cold water. Place them in a large bowl and cover with 4 cups of water. Let it soak for at least 4 hours or overnight.

Strain Hibiscus Infusion:
- After soaking, strain the hibiscus infusion using a fine mesh strainer or cheesecloth, separating the liquid from the petals.

Sweeten the Hibiscus Infusion:
- Pour the hibiscus infusion into a large jug. Add sugar to taste, stirring until the sugar dissolves completely.

Add Fruit Juices:
- Add the pineapple juice and orange juice to the sweetened hibiscus infusion. Stir well to combine.

Chill the Bissap Juice:
- Place the jug in the refrigerator and let the Bissap juice chill for at least 2 hours.

Serve:
- Serve the Bissap juice over ice cubes if desired. Garnish with fresh mint leaves for added freshness.

Enjoy:
- Refresh yourself with the flavorful and vibrant Bissap juice. It can be enjoyed on its own or served as a refreshing accompaniment to meals.

Note:

- Adjust the sweetness according to your preference by adding more or less sugar.
- You can experiment with additional flavors by adding a splash of lime juice or ginger for extra zing.

Bissap juice is known for its vibrant red color and tangy, floral flavor. It is a popular beverage in Senegal and other West African countries, especially during hot weather. The drink is not only delicious but also packed with antioxidants and vitamins from the hibiscus petals and fruit juices.

Chibwantu (Zambia)

Ingredients:

- Ripe marula fruits (quantity according to preference)
- Water
- Sugar (optional, depending on the sweetness of the fruits)
- Large, clean glass or plastic container with a lid

Instructions:

Harvest and Clean Marula Fruits:
- Harvest ripe marula fruits. Ensure they are clean and free from any contaminants.

Remove Seeds:
- Remove the seeds from the marula fruits. You can do this by cutting each fruit in half and scooping out the seeds.

Mash the Fruits:
- Mash the marula fruits using a clean utensil or your hands. The goal is to break down the fruits and release their juices.

Transfer to Container:
- Transfer the mashed marula fruits into a clean, large glass or plastic container with a lid.

Add Water:
- Add enough water to the mashed fruits to cover them. The water will help extract the flavors from the fruits during the fermentation process.

Cover and Ferment:
- Cover the container with a lid and allow the marula mixture to ferment. The fermentation process may take several days to a few weeks, depending on factors like temperature and desired alcohol content.

Strain:
- Once the fermentation is complete, strain the liquid to remove the solid fruit residues. You can use a fine mesh strainer or cheesecloth for this step.

Sweeten (Optional):
- Taste the liquid and, if desired, add sugar to sweeten the Chibwantu. Stir well to ensure the sugar is fully dissolved.

Bottle and Store:
- Pour the strained Chibwantu into clean bottles with tight-fitting lids. Seal the bottles and store them in a cool, dark place.

Maturation:
- Allow the Chibwantu to mature for a few more days or weeks. This maturation period enhances the flavors and allows the drink to develop its characteristic taste.

Serve Chilled:
- Once the Chibwantu has matured, chill it in the refrigerator before serving.

Enjoy Responsibly:
- Serve Chibwantu chilled and enjoy this traditional Zambian beverage responsibly.

Note:

- Chibwantu is an alcoholic beverage, so it's important to consume it responsibly and be aware of its alcohol content.
- The sweetness of the Chibwantu can be adjusted by adding more or less sugar during the sweetening step.

Chibwantu is not only a beverage but also a part of Zambian cultural traditions, often consumed during celebrations and special occasions. The use of locally available fruits, like marula, adds a unique and regional touch to this traditional drink.

Amagwinya/Vetkoek (South Africa)

Ingredients:

- 4 cups all-purpose flour
- 2 tablespoons sugar
- 1 teaspoon salt
- 1 packet (10g) instant yeast
- 1 1/2 cups lukewarm water
- Cooking oil for deep frying

Instructions:

Prepare the Dough:
- In a large mixing bowl, combine the all-purpose flour, sugar, and salt.

Activate the Yeast:
- In a separate bowl, dissolve the instant yeast in lukewarm water. Let it sit for a few minutes until it becomes frothy.

Make the Dough:
- Pour the activated yeast mixture into the dry ingredients. Mix to form a soft dough. Knead the dough on a floured surface until it is smooth and elastic.

Let the Dough Rise:
- Place the dough back in the mixing bowl, cover it with a clean kitchen towel, and let it rise in a warm place for about 1 hour or until it has doubled in size.

Heat Oil for Frying:
- In a deep fryer or a large, deep pot, heat cooking oil to 350°F (180°C).

Shape and Fry:
- Divide the risen dough into golf ball-sized portions. Flatten each portion slightly to form discs or rounds.
- Carefully place the shaped dough into the hot oil, frying a few at a time. Fry until the amagwinya are golden brown on both sides, turning as needed. This usually takes about 3-4 minutes per side.

Drain Excess Oil:
- Once fried, use a slotted spoon to remove the amagwinya from the oil. Place them on a plate lined with paper towels to drain any excess oil.

Serve:
- Serve amagwinya warm. They can be enjoyed on their own or filled with various toppings or fillings, such as polony, cheese, mince, or jam.

Amagwinya are versatile and can be enjoyed as a snack or a meal, depending on the filling. They are a popular street food and a beloved treat at gatherings and events in South Africa. Feel free to get creative with the fillings and enjoy these delicious, deep-fried delights.

Nsima (Malawi)

Ingredients:

- 2 cups maize flour (cornmeal)
- 4-5 cups water
- A pinch of salt (optional)

Instructions:

Boil Water:
- In a large, heavy-bottomed pot, bring 4 cups of water to a boil.

Mix Maize Flour with Water:
- In a separate bowl, mix the maize flour with the remaining 1 cup of water to create a smooth, thick paste. Ensure there are no lumps.

Add Maize Paste to Boiling Water:
- Carefully add the maize paste to the boiling water, stirring continuously to prevent lumps from forming.

Stir Vigorously:
- Continue stirring the mixture vigorously to avoid any lumps. It should start to thicken.

Reduce Heat and Simmer:
- Reduce the heat to low and let the mixture simmer. Use a wooden spoon to continue stirring and breaking up any lumps that may form.

Cook Until Thickened:
- Cook the nsima for about 10-15 minutes or until it reaches a thick, dough-like consistency. It should be smooth and free of lumps.

Adjust Consistency:
- If the nsima is too thick, you can add a bit more hot water and continue stirring until you achieve the desired consistency. If it's too thin, you can add more maize flour.

Season with Salt (Optional):
- If desired, add a pinch of salt to taste and stir it into the nsima.

Serve:
- Once the nsima is cooked to the right consistency, remove it from the heat. Use a wooden spoon or a traditional utensil called a "ntelele" to scoop and shape the nsima into portions.

Serve Warm:
- Serve nsima warm alongside a variety of dishes, such as vegetable stews, meats, or fish.

Nsima is a fundamental part of the Malawian diet, and it is often enjoyed with relishes or sauces made from vegetables, legumes, or meats. The way nsima is eaten may vary, with people using their hands to scoop and shape it into bite-sized portions before dipping it into the accompanying relish. It is a versatile and filling dish that is deeply rooted in the culinary traditions of Malawi and neighboring regions.

www.ingramcontent.com/pod-product-compliance
Lightning Source LLC
LaVergne TN
LVHW081552060526
838201LV00054B/1871